The
Literature
Review

SIX
STEPS
TO
SUCCESS

The
Literature
Review

LAWRENCE A. MACHI

BRENDA T. McEVOY

CORWIN
PRESS
A SAGE Company

For information:

Corwin Press
A SAGE Company
2455 Teller Road
Thousand Oaks, California 91320
www.corwinpress.com

SAGE Ltd.
1 Oliver's Yard
55 City Road
London EC1Y 1SP
United Kingdom

SAGE India Pvt. Ltd.
B 1/I 1 Mohan Cooperative
   Industrial Area
Mathura Road, New Delhi 110 044
India

SAGE Asia-Pacific Pte. Ltd.
33 Pekin Street #02-01
Far East Square
Singapore 048763

Printed in the United States of America.

Library of Congress Cataloging-in-Publication Data

Machi, Lawrence A.
The literature review: six steps to success/Lawrence A. Machi, Brenda T. McEvoy.
    p. cm.
Includes bibliographical references and index.
ISBN 978-1-4129-6134-9 (cloth : acid-free paper)
ISBN 978-1-4129-6135-6 (pbk. : acid-free paper)
    1. Research—Methodology—Study and teaching (Secondary)—Handbooks, manuals, etc. 2. Research—Methodology—Study and teaching (Higher)—Handbooks, manuals, etc. 3. Research—Methodology—Handbooks, manuals, etc. I. McEvoy, Brenda T. II. Title.

LB1047.3.M33 2009
001.4—dc22   2008019170

This book is printed on acid-free paper.

08   09   10   11   12   10   9   8   7   6   5   4   3   2   1

Acquisitions Editor:	Debra Stollenwerk
Editorial Assistant:	Allison Scott
Production Editor:	Eric Garner
Copy Editor:	Alison Hope
Typesetter:	C&M Digitals (P) Ltd.
Proofreader:	Caryne Brown
Indexer:	Ellen Slavitz
Cover Designer:	Michael Dubowe

Contents

Preface

This book is organized as a road map for researching, arguing, and composing a literature review. Doing a literature review is a complex project for even the most advanced researcher, especially if learning how to compose a literature review has been by trial and error. To become successful at this craft, researchers need many skills. They need a way to narrow the research topic and to focus their literature search, and they need the tools necessary to negotiate the myriad books, periodicals, and reports about their topic. Therefore, the purpose of this book is to gather into one volume the strategies, tools, and techniques of the experienced researcher.

AUDIENCE

Those new to research can use this text to learn their craft, while more advanced students may use it as a means to review their skills, and perhaps pick up some new tips. This book is intended for use by two groups of researchers: those completing master's theses, and those working on doctoral dissertations. If you are doing a class assignment or completing most master's degree projects, the text will address the type of literature review that summarizes and evaluates the existing knowledge on a particular topic. Some master's theses, and all doctoral dissertations, require a more sophisticated literature review. This book also addresses this type of literature review that uses preliminary library (or Internet) research to argue and define a problem that requires original research.

While this book uses education as its context, the model, strategies, and tools presented apply to a much wider audience within the social sciences. Because education is an applied science, many of the examples and strategies contained in the book consider the literature from a variety of vantage points including social and organizational psychology, sociology, and group psychology. Thus, students studying these disciplines will also find this text helpful.

SPECIAL FEATURES AND TEXT ORGANIZATION

All students, beginning or advanced, can use a straightforward guide for maneuvering through the ambiguities of framing the topic, managing information, developing the argument, and acquiring the composition skills needed to produce a successful literature review. There are definite tricks of the trade for making this project an efficient and enjoyable experience. This text is organized around a six-step literature review model to guide the reader through the project. These steps follow:

- Step 1. Select a topic.
- Step 2. Search the literature.
- Step 3. Develop the argument.
- Step 4. Survey the literature.
- Step 5. Critique the literature.
- Step 6. Write the review.

Each chapter addresses a specific step of the model and contains several learning aids to increase reader comprehension. These learning aids include the following:

- Exercises that work the reader through the more involved procedures. These guided practice opportunities and examples aid in checking understanding.
- Technology references that suggest software that can simplify the work of organizing material and revising the written composition.
- Graphics and charts that clarify the key topics under discussion, and models that present pictures that tie together complex themes and procedures.
- At the end of each chapter, tips provide specific ideas for using the material covered in the chapter. These tips will help the reader make immediate, practical use of the material.

- Each chapter has a summary that gives a brief recap of the chapter's contents and acts as an aid when a reader wishes to review information.
- Finally, each chapter closes with a checklist. These lists allow readers to track their progress through the entire literature review project.
- At the end of the text, the reader can refer to the glossary for definitions of often-used terms and to a reference list of works for further reading.

When you confront the task of successfully producing a literature review, you have two choices: Either you can proceed in an organized fashion using a book such as this one to guide your endeavors, or you can plunge blindly into the project trying to find the time and resources needed, while crossing your fingers and hoping for the best. Experienced researchers know that trial and error is frustrating and time consuming, and rarely successful. Learning the key ideas in this text will save you from frustration and lost time.

Acknowledgments

Corwin Press gratefully acknowledges the contributions of the following reviewers:

Scott McLeod
Director
UCEA Center for the
   Advanced Study of
   Technology Leadership
   in Education (CASTLE)
Iowa State University
Ames, IA

Richard D. Kellough
Professor Emeritus
California State University
Sacramento, CA

William G. Camp, PhD
Professor, Department of
   Education
Cornell University
Ithaca, NY

David Freitas, EdD
Professor
School of Education
Indiana, University South Bend
South Bend, IN

Carl A. Grant
Professor
University Wisconsin-Madison
Madison, WI

About the Authors

Lawrence A. Machi is a professor in the Department of Organizational Leadership at the University of La Verne, in La Verne, California. He holds an MA in curriculum development, and an EdD in organizational leadership. He teaches research methods and design, and chairs doctoral dissertation research in addition to teaching classes in organizational development. Machi has extensive experience in higher education, and has taught in schools of education at the University of San Francisco, St. Mary's College of California, and Sonoma State University prior to his tenure at La Verne.

Machi has also been a K–12 educator. He has worked as a secondary teacher and served as a school administrator in secondary and elementary school districts in Northern California. He has occupied the roles of vice principal, principal, assistant superintendent, and superintendent.

Machi has consulted with many California school districts and nonprofit organizations over the years. His specialties are in the areas of finance, negotiations, and organizational development.

Brenda T. McEvoy began her fascination with research and writing when she was the "interested amateur" reader for her father's books on topics ranging from Pueblo ethnology to natural history, from fifteen to twenty years old. Those five years of early experience taught her the importance of careful research in producing logical arguments expressed in clear, understandable language. She has taught high school English and history for the past thirty years. Research skills are always part of her curriculum.

For eight years, she worked for the California State Department of Education leading groups of educators in improving their ability to edit and assess student writing. Also for the state, she was a mentor for beginning English and history teachers. Participation in the California Writing Project extended her knowledge of writing and the difficulties that students at all levels face when producing a major assignment. She has worked as an editor and a proofreader for the books of several associates. She is currently doing research on health insurance coverage for two teachers' associations. Her depth of experience as a practitioner teaching writing and researching at many levels has shown her the many pitfalls that can bedevil student researchers. Her major interest has always been to help writers create work that is clear and logical. This continuing professional focus coupled with experience is a natural fit for creating a book that guides student researchers toward producing literature reviews that are well researched, well argued, and well written.

Introduction

The Literature Review Process

Getting Started

Chi ha fretta vada piano.
In order to go fast, you must go slow.

So you need to produce a **literature review**. Perhaps this is a class assignment, a thesis for a master's degree, or the foundation for your doctoral dissertation. Whether you are approaching this task as a first-time or experienced researcher, you are doing it for the same reason: to increase your skills and knowledge. You want to learn, and you also want the satisfaction of completing a job well. To succeed, you will want to avoid the problem mentioned by one of our colleagues: "Some do not have the patience and foresight to do it right the first time, but have the infinite patience and capacity to do it over, and over, and over again."

The good news is that you do not need to "reinvent" the literature review process. You do not have to use trial and error. There are known procedures and skills you can use to make your task easier and more efficient. This book provides a road map to guide you in producing a literature review that will contribute to your field. If you use this text conscientiously, it will help you arrive successfully at your destination. It offers tips and tools from many sources, including from the authors' experience. Using this information should enable you to plan your literature review journey to your own satisfaction, without losing time and effort with wrong turns and detours.

This introductory chapter begins with the selection of your destination—that is, with the selection of your literature review's purpose. As you begin, ask yourself, "Am I trying to present a thesis that defines the current state of knowledge about a **topic**, or am I arguing a thesis that defines a research problem for further study?"

THE PURPOSE OF A LITERATURE REVIEW

Literature reviews have different purposes depending on the nature of the inquiry. If the purpose of the inquiry is to advance a position about the current state of knowledge on a topic, then you are doing a basic literature review. If the purpose of the inquiry is to uncover a research problem for further study, then you are doing an advanced literature review.

The basic literature review (Figure I.1) summarizes and evaluates the existing knowledge on a particular topic. Its purpose is to produce a position on the state of that knowledge; this is the thesis.

The basic literature review begins when you select and identify a research **interest** or issue for inquiry; this is the study question.

Figure I.1   The Basic Literature Review

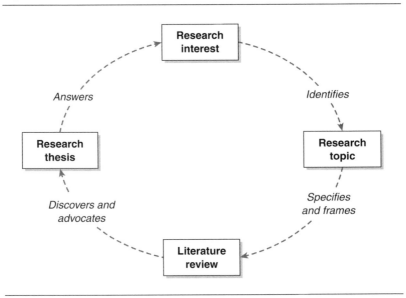

As you proceed, you will narrow and clarify this question into a research topic. The research topic specifies and frames the literature review. The outcome of the literature review will be the discovery and advocacy of a research thesis, which answers the study question. For instance, a class assignment or master's degree thesis would require a basic literature review.

The advanced literature review (Figure I.2) takes the inquiry one step further. It, too, selects a research interest and research topic; then it reviews the literature, leading to a research thesis. At that point, it proposes further research, which leads to identifying a research project, the determination of which leads to research findings and conclusions. The advanced literature review is the foundation for identifying a problem that demands original research, and is the basis for the study of a research problem.

In the advanced literature review, the researcher first addresses the current state of knowledge about the study question. Then, based on these findings, the researcher proposes a thesis that defines an

Figure I.2   The Advanced Literature Review

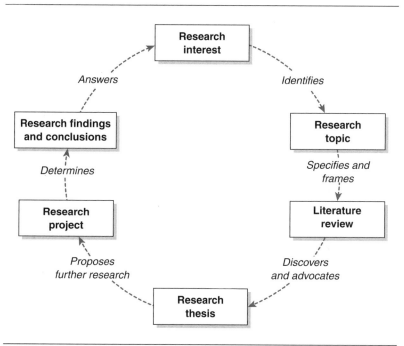

issue for further study. Advanced master's theses and all doctoral dissertations use the advanced literature review as a stepping-stone for discovering what is not yet known about the topic.

While basic reviews and advanced reviews seek different outcomes, the manner by which they uncover knowledge and produce a thesis are similar and parallel.

THE LITERATURE REVIEW DEFINED

A literature review is a written **argument** that promotes a thesis position by building a case from credible **evidence** based on previous research. It provides the context and the background about the current knowledge of the topic and lays out a logical case to defend the thesis position taken. Here is our definition of a literature review:

> *A literature review is a written document that presents a logically argued case founded on a comprehensive understanding of the current state of knowledge about a topic of study. This case establishes a convincing thesis to answer the study's question.*

THE LITERATURE REVIEW PROCESS

A literature review is an organized way to research the chosen topic. Figure I.3 shows the steps for conducting a literature review.

Writing a literature review is developmental, with each of the six steps leading to the next (Figure I.3). The following is a brief explanation of the six steps:

Step 1. Select a Topic

A successful research topic is usually the result of an interest in a practical problem. That interest must move from everyday language into ideas that form a researchable topic. This topic must be stated as a well-defined question accessible to a specific academic discipline. Specifying the language, refining the focus of the interest, and selecting the academic vantage point are the tasks necessary to create a research topic. The result is a defined topic that provides the direction for Step 2.

Figure I.3   The Literature Review Model

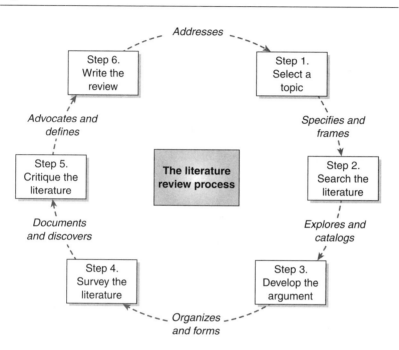

Step 2. Search the Literature

A **literature search** determines what information will be in the review. It does this by winnowing the information to only the **data** that provide the strongest evidence to support the thesis. When searching the literature, you must preview, select, and organize the data for study by using the skills of **skimming**, **scanning**, and **mapping** the data. At this point, you catalog and document the relevant data.

Step 3. Develop the Argument

To argue your thesis successfully, you need to form and then present your case. To form your case, you need to arrange your **claims** logically. To present your case, you need to organize the relevant data into a body of evidence that explains what is known about the topic.

Step 4. Survey the Literature

The **literature survey** assembles, synthesizes, and analyzes the data to form the argument about the current knowledge on the topic. The evidence creates a logical and defensible set of conclusions or claims. These conclusions provide the basis for addressing the research question.

Step 5. Critique the Literature

The **literature critique** interprets the current understanding of the topic. It analyzes how previous knowledge answers the research question.

Step 6. Write the Review

Thesis writing transforms the research project into a document for others. Through composing, molding, and refining, the written literature review becomes a work that accurately conveys the research and that can be understood by the intended audience. Thesis writing requires writing, **auditing**, and editing to produce a polished final composition.

The above discussion of the literature review, although condensed, provides a preliminary understanding of what you already know and what you still need to learn about the literature review. The succeeding chapters will describe the specifics for each step and help you to complete each of the tasks necessary for building a strong thesis position and conducting a good review. We turn now to a discussion of fundamentals—inquiry, researcher mind-set, and planning.

INQUIRY: THE NECESSARY PRECONDITION

All successful research begins with inquiry. The researcher must have an inquiring mind, natural curiosity, and a fundamental need to learn and discover. The researcher must have an innate awareness of when present knowledge is insufficient and must have an intuitive sense of when something is missing.

- Curiosity creates the sparks that ignite a need to explore what lies beyond the currently known. This fire, in turn, sprouts the seeds that are the fragile beginnings of the research itself. Inquiring researchers begin their work with questions: "Why? What if . . . ? Is it true?" These questions and others like them are the bedrock of research; without them there is no good research.

- The inquiring researcher knows that each person has biases, opinions, beliefs, values, and experiences that come together to create a unique perspective. While these are fundamental human traits, researchers set them aside during the research process. Ideally, personal perspective should have no influence on the researcher's thinking and no place in the conduct of the research.

- The inquiring researcher comes to the research with an open mind. This researcher is objective, champions no favorites, and has no predetermined conclusions. This researcher is open to seeing all results of the inquiry, has no agenda, and weighs the value of each piece of evidence.

- The inquiring researcher looks at the evidence with a keen eye. This researcher looks for nuances when noting data, constantly looking for connections and patterns in the data. The researcher sees both the trees and the forest.

- The inquiring researcher thinks critically and weighs all data for veracity and value. This researcher seeks evidence, examines the pros and cons of any questions, and makes thesis claims based on strong evidence-based arguments.

- The inquiring researcher proceeds with diligence. This inquirer knows that any solid research need many hours of painstaking work. Data identification, collection, cataloging, and documenting need large blocks of time. There are no shortcuts. All good research builds on a thorough investigation of the facts. As any detective knows, successful investigations call for wearing through large quantities of shoe leather.

- The inquiring researcher is deliberate. This researcher acts on a calculated purpose with careful consideration and thoughtful intent. Good research builds on solid thinking and careful execution.

- The inquiring researcher reflects continually. This inquirer advances with skepticism, and questions everything. The research and the researcher are under constant self-scrutiny: "What did I do? What does it mean? How did it work? What should I do next?" The inquiring researcher is constantly learning, reflecting on the past in order to navigate the present while examining the here and now to select the best course forward.

- The inquiring researcher works ethically. Plagiarism of ideas and words is unthinkable. The ethical inquirer acknowledges all who have come before, and understands what Newton meant when he wrote, "If I have seen farther it is by standing on the shoulders of giants."

These behaviors are the building blocks of academic rigor and discipline. Researchers must have rigor and discipline to conduct their tasks successfully. Rigorous and disciplined research, by its nature, must be deliberate and reflective. Researchers must strive to turn over all stones, scrupulously examine everything in their path, and conscientiously report all they find. These behaviors are tools for producing high-quality work, ethical research, and good science. Remember, "In order to go fast, you must go slow."

PACK WISELY BEFORE YOU BEGIN

The secret for any successful journey—and a literature review is a kind of journey—is planning and preparation. The successful researcher must be physically and emotionally ready, and must have a plan of action. Doing a literature review well demands a commitment of focused time and effort, which will probably require a fundamental reorganization of daily life. A project such as a literature review cannot take place "when time allows," because time would probably never allow. Rather than trying to integrate this new work into the already-busy day, you should seek creative scheduling solutions.

First, you should organize a workspace free from distractions. Make sure the space has good lighting and that all necessary tools are conveniently placed. You will need a computer with an Internet connection, copying and printing capability, notepads, writing instruments, and filing space. You will also need, minimally, at least one high-quality dictionary and thesaurus. Reference works on research methods and writing skills can also be useful. Plan the space, and arrange it before you begin.

As with any complex project, the literature review demands concentrated mental focus. Mental discipline demands emotional balance. You must be actively present in mind and in spirit when conducting your work. If pressures invade your mental space, then concentration and focus decrease or disappear. Being contemplative is a strong aid to keeping emotional balance. When beginning a new day's research, start by putting the emotions and the pressures of the day aside; they can return later. Say to yourself that you are present and ready to work, and only then begin. Concentration is everything.

Having a plan increases productivity. Develop a three-level plan. First, create an overall project plan and time line. Second, subdivide the overall plan into sections that act as intermediate goals for the project. Finally, build daily plans from the subsections to schedule the work for each daily session. Remember, a plan implies a goal. Give yourself permission to modify your plan, but never proceed without one. Plans provide direction and organization. They build a structure to address the ambiguous and complex world of the literature review. These are our suggestions for planning:

1. Build an overall plan. Use the literature review model, Figure I.3, to form the overall plan. First, estimate the available monthly research time that you have for the project. Calculate this in hours, then estimate the number of hours it will take to complete the tasks for each step of the literature review. If you are not comfortable assigning task times, consult with colleagues or faculty who are experienced in literature research. Next, build an overall plan and time line for the research. Be sure to include extra time for unplanned eventualities.

2. Subdivide the plan by benchmarks that will serve as intermediate goals for the research. These benchmarks can be time or task driven. A monthly design is one choice if time is the measurement for progress. Use the steps of the literature review model when you use task completion as the measure of progress. Put the benchmarks on a time line, and readjust the overall plan as necessary. The benchmark division drives the work. It provides you with a solid schedule that addresses the tasks. At this point, the work becomes tangible.

3. Build daily plans for action. Each work session must have its goals. Ask yourself each day, "What do I have to do today?" If possible, schedule at least a two-hour block of time for each session. Early morning works best for many, when the house or library is quiet, allowing you to focus and concentrate more easily. Other times of the day may be more suitable in your case. Schedule a time with no interruptions and quiet surroundings. Give yourself enough time to complete a significant amount of work in each session. We recommend daily sessions. While two-hour sessions each day may be impractical, daily work on the project is not. Allowing extended time between work sessions will blur your focus. The literature review is a serious undertaking that builds one day at a time. You cannot succeed by leaving the work for the last minute. Of course, as you use the daily schedule, your benchmarks and the overall plan may need to change.

TIPS

- Study carefully the literature review model (Figure I.3). Memorize it if possible. Use this figure to keep yourself on track.
- Select a topic that is important to you. A subject of true concern or curiosity will produce better work than a topic chosen for expediency.
- Plan every step. Going back to pick up missed steps takes far more time than completing the work diligently.

SUMMARY

The purpose of this chapter is to provide you with a general introduction to both the conduct and the product of a literature review. The chapter provides a discussion of what it means to be an inquirer, and gives a description of the traits of a good researcher. This chapter ends with preparation tips to help you launch a successful literature review. With a preliminary understanding of the project, a thoughtful mind-set, and a plan, you are ready to tackle developing the research topic, which is the subject of Chapter 1.

CHECKLIST	
Task	Completed
1. Are you clear on the definition and purpose of a literature review?	☐
2. Do you have a general interest to begin exploring?	☐
3. Have you internalized the six steps needed to create a successful literature review?	☐
4. Are you physically and emotionally ready to be an inquiring researcher?	☐
5. Do you have a suitable workspace, with necessary tools?	☐
6. Have you built an overall plan?	☐

Select a Topic

Everyday Interest to Research Topic

Chi zappa in fretta, raccoglierà piangendo.
Hoe in haste, harvest in tears.

The Literature Review Model

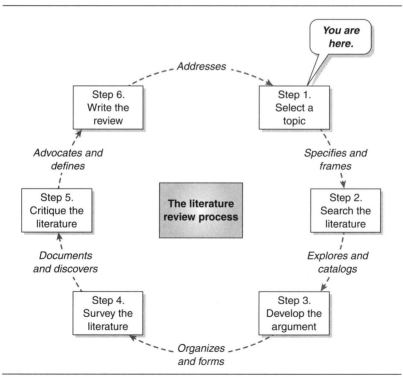

All research begins with curiosity. The origin of most research interests stems from curiosity about the conflicts, issues, concerns, or beliefs about daily work and living. Most research interests come from questioning why specific facets of work succeed while others fail; whether some strategies or tactics succeed more than others; or why people think, learn, and act in certain ways. Questions that could stimulate research are as follows: "What causes the conflict among members of committee work groups?" or "How accurate are standardized test scores in measuring individual student achievement?"

Administrators try to improve organizations by developing better programs, by improving connections among people, and by motivating people to complete specific tasks. For example, what is the recipe for creating successful change? Is a precondition having a forceful leader? How does the principal guide the teaching staff to improve student performance? Is it by "telling it like it is"?

It is helpful, first, to examine this idea called "research interest." Notice that in the examples used the concept is presented in two ways: it names a passion or a concern about some subject, and it names the subject itself. Concern and passion drive the researcher, providing the "why" for the work being considered. The second meaning of interest, the "what" of the research, provides the necessary information for gaining entry into the study. You must define and clarify this "what" of the research until you can identify it in the literature. That is, your everyday interest must be transformed into a researchable topic for study.

How does an everyday interest evolve into a researchable topic for study? For this change to occur, three transformations must take place. The first transformation is one of specificity. When asked to select a research interest, most beginning researchers will answer with a global response, such as, "I am interested in why students are not achieving." The problem with this response lies in its lack of specificity and clarity. Given only this statement, could a researcher see and measure the concern? Of course not. The interest, as expressed, is too broad, lacking the specificity needed to view it. To provide clarity, you must provide a more detailed description of the subject under study. The interest must be specific, and it must be precise. An example of an everyday interest is, "How does the weather change from season to season?" A researchable interest might be, "To what degree is March weather in coastal northern California influenced by an Arctic flow of air?" Which of these two interests would be easier to research—the general or the specific? Clearly, only the specific can be a subject of research.

The second transformation is one of focus. Is the defined interest too complicated, or does this interest contain multiple subjects for study? By focusing on simplicity and choice, you focus on the interest. You must choose one subject to study, one that can be examined clearly. You must set clear boundaries. Have you chosen a subject that you can clearly describe and singularly define? Research interests need to focus on one subject of study. Instead of the earlier example, "I am interested in why students are not achieving," try, "What effect does understanding specific academic language have on achievement in the natural sciences for third-grade Hispanic second-language learners?"

The third transformation you must make is one of perspective. The everyday interest comes from a personal vantage point, which is your personal need to know more about a specific subject. A researchable interest emerges from the vantage point of an academic discipline, and from an academic field's need to know. The research topic unfolds from that academic field's scholarly writings and questions posed in academic conversation and debate about that subject. You must approach your work using a specific academic vantage point. Doing so provides a direct avenue along which specific knowledge of your topic can be accessed.

A personal interest is not necessarily significant to the larger research community. Your personal concern must also be a concern for the larger academic community. The research interest must address the academic field's need to know and must be a question for the entire academic community to consider. We often have to ask our students, "Does your curiosity, your need to know about something, mean that the scientific community has that same need?" Often, a personal need to know can be satisfied by simply reading the research of others. Usable research must further current knowledge in the field through both a synthesis of present knowledge and an original contribution extending that knowledge. Framing a solid research interest is the key that unlocks the doors to the research literature and opens access to the research topic.

The topic is more than simply the main idea of a paper. The topic provides the entry point to the academic discussion surrounding the research interest, decides the setting of the literature review, identifies the subject of research, and defines the boundary for the logical argument that will be necessary. Organize and synthesize the data found in order to make a case for what is known about the subject under study, and sometimes also to prove what else needs to be studied.

Selecting a topic involves three stages (Figure 1.1):

1. Choose a research interest.

2. Select a research interest from the everyday interest.

3. Use the research interest to choose the research topic.

Figure 1.1   Selecting The Topic

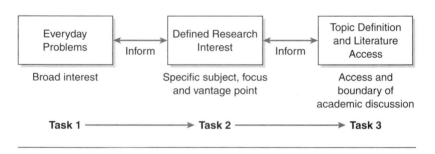

STAGE 1. CHOOSE A RESEARCH INTEREST

Most applied research begins when you select an everyday problem, interest, or concern for further study. Selecting an interest for study needs great care and forethought. As our opening quote says, "Hoe in haste, harvest in tears." Selecting a suitable interest for research is critical to the success of the project. This search begins with personal reflection that uncovers an interest.

We have made the case that research interests come mainly from experience. Various professional and public settings provide the context for these experiences and provide fruitful opportunities for the discovery of issues leading to a research topic. Researchers can introspectively uncover personal issues about their professional experiences. If one's own issues do not readily come to mind, other avenues are available. You can ask for topic suggestions from experts knowledgeable in the academic disciplines or from those who are skilled practitioners in the field. Perhaps reading the various academic and professional trade journals could uncover areas for further research; frequently, journal articles close with suggestions for further research. Tapping into media and professional association reports about current issues in your field will also present research alternatives. The current national, state, or local debates and initiatives addressing your professional field can also become research interests. Finally, you can seek issues from your applied field and identify the scientific principles or theories of the social sciences to discover what implications those principles and theories would have in solving the problem.

For example, what theories in cognitive psychology speak to the developmental learning abilities of students? What does sociological theory propose about group behavior? How does cultural anthropological theory provide an understanding about the culture of the work community? The theoretical models in the various social sciences can always provide new insights. In fact, there are many places to find research interests:

- Professional experience
- Suggestions from experts
- Academic journals
- Media

Researchers study issues or concerns that have important outcomes for the lives of those in their work community. These issues and concerns stem from programs, interactions, and behaviors that are not working. You will want to fix these problems. At first blush they may appear clear cut, but when examined closely, it will be clear that they consist of many parts and levels of human interaction. These concerns are complex and multidimensional. We seek simple explanations and simple fixes for these important issues, but the quick fix seldom presents itself. The solutions for these problems will be developed from a collection of factual data presented from multiple perspectives and vantage points. The secret to selecting a researchable interest is to isolate a particular perspective and vantage point.

Exercises

Throughout this text, you will find a series of exercises to help you in the various tasks of developing a literature review. The first four exercises will employ both brainstorming and free writes. A *brainstorming* or *free write* is spontaneous writing done without reference to notes or outlines. Its purpose is to explore what the writer has already internalized about a subject. Your introspection will address four topics in four free write exercises, each of which will appear at the end of this chapter's subsections. The topic statement for each exercise is followed by guiding questions to help you free write. Respond to each question by recording your ideas as they occur to you. These ideas are the content of your free write. Apply the directions given below to the exercises found at the end of the next four subsections.

- The following guiding questions will help in specifying your interest and surfacing your personal attachments. These questions should pinpoint an interest and identify your personal connection with the interest you wish to study. Each exercise has a set of probing questions that will allow you to explore your interest from a different perspective. Each of these questions is the subject of one free write exercise.
- Use a separate sheet of paper for each session. Copy the topic and the questions for that exercise at the head of the paper, then answer each question in descending order. Read the question aloud, then act quickly, allowing ideas and responses to flow. As ideas come to mind, write them as simple, independent declarative statements, one after the other, as quickly as you can. Do not be concerned with spelling, grammar, or development.
- Allow no more than about fifteen minutes for each session. If you have exhausted your responses to the questions before the end of fifteen minutes, wait for about thirty seconds, and push yourself to find three more responses. After the exercise, put the paper down without rereading it, and leave it for about a day. At the end of the twenty-four-hour period, go back to your writing for that exercise. Read, review, edit, delete, and add whatever comes to mind. Follow this pattern for the exercise in each of the next four subsections.

EXERCISE 1.1

Discovering the Subject of My Interest or Issue of Inquiry

1. What is my research interest or issue?

2. What are its parts?

3. What are the key ideas that make up the interest?

Researcher Bias

As well as picking significant issues for study, you often have personal attachments and views about an issue. Researchers have opinions about the problems in their field, and pet answers to which they are committed. These preconceptions, personal attachments, and views present both pluses and minuses to the research effort. Personal attachment to an interest provides the passion and dedication necessary for conducting good research, which is a plus. Unfortunately, personal attachment also carries bias and opinion that can cause a researcher to jump to conclusions rather than arrive at a conclusion after methodical scholarly work. While your bias and opinion can never be completely removed, they must be controlled.

How does a researcher control bias and opinion? First, careful introspection can bring these views and attachments to the forefront, where they can be identified as what they are. By rationally identifying and confronting these views, you can control personal bias, opinion, and preferred outcome, and can become open minded, skeptical, and considerate of research data. If these attachments remain embedded and unidentified as what they are, the research will be severely compromised. A biased researcher can only produce biased findings. The key to selecting an interest is dependent on the ability to remain objective and to narrow the focus of a practical interest to a tangible research subject without leaving behind the personal passion to follow a particular line of study.

EXERCISE 1.2

Understanding the Personal Viewpoint

1. What previous knowledge do you have about your interest?

2. What personal experience do you have that influences you about this issue or interest?

3. What are your beliefs, biases, and opinions about this interest or issue?

4. What predisposes you to certain conclusions about the issue or concern of study?

5. How will you identify and isolate your personal bias, opinion, feelings, and intuition to preserve your neutral position as a researcher?

This exercise should have disclosed some potential demons. Demons are unavoidable, but they must not control or influence the research. They can, however, be a point of entry to the significance, the "why" of the research. Put them to work when you explore the significance of the research.

STAGE 2. SELECT A RESEARCH INTEREST FROM THE EVERYDAY INTEREST

Selecting a potential issue for research is just the first stage in Step 1. Next you must narrow the selected interest down to a clearly identifiable, significant, researchable interest. The first formation of a research interest is seldom suitable for study. Often, early considerations of a research interest are so broad that subject specificity, focus, and vantage point are, at best, ill defined. Much work is necessary to give your first interest the specificity needed to develop a research topic. What do you actually want to study? Is it well defined? What focus will you use to examine it? Where—from what angle or vantage point—can you best conduct the research? You must clearly define your potential research interest. You must select a specific focus and vantage point. There are many studies within each broad interest that can provide important contributions; the trick is to settle on one. So what subject actually interests you? What is your point of view on that subject? What approach will you take? Begin by addressing subject specificity.

Specifying a Research Interest

Is your original interest clearly defined? The key to clearly defining the topic depends on your ability to isolate the key ideas in the statement of interest. The subject of any research is defined by the key ideas—those words and phases that create meaning for the interest statement. Broad interests tend to be ambiguous and are not suitable for research. A broad first interest statement includes many inferred key ideas that need definition. Precise topic definition is necessary. The following demonstrates the problem.

An example of a research interest used earlier in this chapter was, "To what degree are standardized test scores predictive of true student achievement?" This is an important question whose answer could contribute to education in significant ways, but it needs to be refined before it can produce a usable topic for study. The broad scope and lack of a clear description of its key ideas demand more consideration before we can gain the specificity needed. What are the key ideas? To identify them, look first for the subjects, verbs, and objects. In this interest statement, the subject is "test scores," the verb is "are," and the object is "predictive [of] achievement." The key idea to be examined, then, then, is "the degree to which test scores are predictive of achievement." When taking apart this first interest statement, it quickly becomes clear that it is too broad. What does *degree* mean? How can you measure it? What does a standardized test assess? How does it measure it? How accurate are the yardsticks of measurement? How do we account for the test's reliability and validity? What does the word "predictive" mean? How can we measure it? What does student achievement look like? We need to become more precise. Unless the statement is refined, you simply have no place to start.

Developing exact definitions for each of the key ideas that make up the interest statement is your first task. Definitions for **key terms** must be exact in order to identify the subject of the research. Without precise definitions, you will not be able to form your topic.

Once you have specified your subject, you need to decide on a focus for your research by focusing the interest.

Focusing the Interest

Focusing the interest means narrowing the study to one clearly defined subject. If the subject is unclear, then you have not determined what is actually being examined. Often, broad interests contain multiple subjects that could be studied. The previous example is one such case. This interest could be studied from an individual, group, or organizational perspective. For instance, the research perspective could focus on the student, specifically individual student behavior, attitude, skills, or knowledge. "How can a change of student behavior affect performance on an achievement test?" "How do student attitudes affect performance in certain achievement assessments?" Alternatively, the research perspective could focus on group behavior. How does a certain group respond to certain testing conditions? What are the effects of this kind of test on group performance?

After narrowing the focus of the broad interest, we see usable topics such as, "To what degree are state standardized test scores in language arts predictive of student success in college placement with regard to <Subject A> exams?" "How does teacher competency in test preparation of students affect student achievement on a standardized test?"

EXERCISE 1.3

Selecting the Focus of Your Study

1. Have you clearly identified the focus of the study interest?

2. Are you looking at individuals, groups, or organizations?

3. Have you specifically named the individuals, groups, or organizations that you plan to study?

The above exercise produced many choices as possible focuses for research. The next step is to narrow the interest to choose one for study.

Selecting a Perspective

Once you have selected the focus of the subject, you need to select the perspective or vantage point, which is the place from which you view the subject. Vantage point results from the choice of an academic discipline, which in turn usually depends on the subject you have chosen to study, and the particular perspective from which you have chosen to study it. Using our example, are you looking at the tribal behavior of groups as it relates to the process of standardized testing and student achievement, or at the environmental or social interactions that affect student achievement and the standardized testing environment? Each of these questions anticipates the need for a particular field of knowledge. If you study achievement from the individual student's perspective, then psychology will provide the best vantage point. If you study achievement from a tribal perspective, then cultural anthropology will provide the best vantage point. If you study achievement from the perspective of group reactions and interactions, then sociology will provide the best vantage point. When you have clearly defined the **core ideas** contained in the interest and determined a specific focus and vantage point from which to study, you will have traveled from the broad everyday interest to a researchable interest.

EXERCISE 1.4

Choosing the Vantage Point for the Study

1. What academic fields best lend themselves to your subject and perspective for research? (If you are still considering more than one perspective, choose a suitable academic field for each perspective.)

2. What are the specific knowledge areas of this academic field that will best help in exploring and defining the research subject?

3. What knowledge competency do you have in this academic field?

4. What more academic field knowledge will you have to acquire to have a solid foundation to address this interest?

As with the focus, you must narrow your vantage point. Many possibilities probably surfaced from the previous exercise. Select the vantage point that will present the best viewpoint for accessing data about the research interest.

Reflection: The Key to Interest Selection

The key to developing a successful potential research topic is your ability to examine the everyday interest, concern, or problem that you select for study. Use personal introspection for this important examination. The more clarity and specificity that you are able to bring to bear, the easier it is to connect this interest to a researchable topic of study.

Experience with students choosing interests tells us that beginning researchers sometimes neglect to take the time necessary for reflecting on what they will actually study. Capturing an interest of study haphazardly without considering intent, perspective, or vantage point can produce awkward and unsatisfactory results.

Taking time to choose your interest for study carefully is critical for all researchers. Remember, "Be careful what you wish for, because you might get it." Don't be too hasty to select an interest. An interest chosen too quickly will often produce a project that is ill defined, and that might well go beyond your research scope and skill.

Taking an everyday interest and transforming it into a usable researchable interest is much like the work of setting up a photograph. Compare selecting a subject for research to photographing a scene. Imagine yourself standing at Big Rock Campground in Joshua Tree National Park. Around you are miles of desert, and shifting light and shadow. Perhaps there are also people, reptiles, plants, cacti, or insects in your scene. Do you want a photo of an ancient juniper tree, or do you want a picture of a family around a campfire? What is the purpose of the photograph, and what is your goal? If your goal is to record the entire park in seasons over time, you would set yourself up for a lifetime's work. Usually, though, your job is not to photograph the entire park or to study everything about your subject, from all perspectives. Rather, it is to select one worthy subject of interest and to do it justice, from your chosen perspective.

For both the photographer and the researcher, an initial interest in the subject sparks the task. In both cases, we have a specific image of the outcome that we expect to see. Also, in both cases that early expectation will, in all likelihood, be different from what actually results. The selection of the subject of a photograph is just a starting point. A satisfactory end product will appear only after much exploration into focus, intent, and perspective, all of which will change as you delve deeper into your subject. Perhaps the final photo will be substantially different from how you originally conceived it. In both photography and research, it is necessary to be willing to see what actually works and to continue down productive paths, while being willing to abandon those paths that meander aimlessly without leading you to satisfactory results. Your first photograph may be of a jagged rock. The photo you keep may be a close-up of the quartz fragments in one section of metamorphic stone in that jagged rock.

Like the photographer, a researcher must have a subject of interest that launches the inquiry, and must also craft and mold the research. The researcher follows a path that works to define the research interest rather than simply adhering to the original intent. Evidence, whether of the eye or the mind, must lead the way.

EXERCISE 1.5

Developing Your Interest Statement

In this exercise, you will combine and pattern the information gathered from your brainstorming and free writes. Reflect on and analyze the information produced by the earlier exercises, and develop a specific statement of interest. This statement could be a single question or a declarative statement. Make it clear and concise. Develop a second statement that defines the significance of the research. Finally, write a statement that clearly defines beliefs, values, biases, and opinions, noting how you will neutralize them when following your research.

Using the information you have developed through your introspective work produced in Exercises 1.1 through 1.4, answer the following three questions.

1. What is your specific research interest?
   a. The interest, issue, or concern of my research is ... [expressed in seven sentences].
   b. Cross out the two least important sentences without changing the key idea.
   c. Cross out any words or phrases that can be removed without changing the meaning.
   d. Reduce your remaining draft to three sentences.
   e. Be sure your final three sentences do the following: Identify the subject (What are you studying?), perspective (How are you looking at it?), and vantage point (What academic field will you use?).

(Continued)

(Continued)

2. What contributions make this research important?

3. What are your beliefs, values, biases, and opinions?

   a. How will these beliefs, values, biases, and opinions help you in conducting your research?

   b. How will you prevent the tendencies contained in your personal viewpoint from affecting your neutral stance as a researcher?

Now, using your answers for Questions 1 through 3, write a statement that clearly defines the interest for your research work, a statement that defines the significance of your research, and a statement that defines your personal tendencies and how you will control them. When completed, you will have a researchable interest.

STAGE 3. USE THE RESEARCH INTEREST TO CHOOSE THE RESEARCH TOPIC

You are now ready to address the last concern of this chapter. How do you translate a defined personal interest of study into a suitable topic for formal research? Begin by reviewing your progress so far.

Figure 1.2 shows the three stages for refining an everyday problem into a usable topic for research. Reading from left to right, notice that in Stage 1 you select an interest that you have identified as an important everyday problem needing attention. If the interest definition is vague, you must clarify it through specific definition. Next, continue to Stage 2.

Your introspection narrows the interest through the choice of a particular subject, perspective, and vantage point. By choosing a vantage point of study, access becomes available to a defined academic field of study. You can now address the final stage for selecting a potential topic of study, which is the last concern of this chapter.

When addressing Stage 3 of Figure 1.2, you leave the personal domain of refining the interest, and enter the formal world of academia. Reframe the defined topic from the subject definition, switching

Figure 1.2   Moving From Interest to Topic

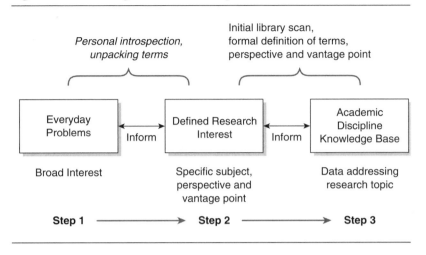

from everyday language to the technical terminology used in a particular academic discipline. At this point, you are moving from the pursuit of an everyday investigation to beginning a formal literature review. At this critical point, you need to translate the statement of interest into a potential topic for formal research. As stated earlier in this chapter, you must align your interest to the external concern and work of that academic community. Why is this important? Without aligning the personal research interest to a topic of study being addressed by the academic community, you have no avenue by which to gain access and entry to the relevant academic body of knowledge.

Often, students believe that they have a well-defined study interest that they call a topic—but we disagree. These students complain that they have been to the library and worked hard at gathering information about their topic, but can find nothing written on it. Rarely does a researcher stumble onto a unique and previously unidentified topic of study. Previous work has been done on almost all the interests we will consider. So what is the difficulty? Usually the difficulty is a lack of academic terminology. Students often try to use their everyday vocabulary to access the language and discourse of a specialized field.

Word usage and meaning are particular to context. All academic fields have an esoteric language to describe their subjects of study.

At its worst, the language deteriorates into jargon. The chances are remote that a researcher's use of everyday language conforms to the technical language used by an academic field. The following example shows the differences in the meaning of a term as used by different academic disciplines.

Consider the word "conflict." Informally, *conflict* is defined as a disagreement or argument, or as an incompatibility of goals between parties. As used in the discipline of history, *conflict* could mean a war, as in an armed conflict. As used in organizational psychology, *conflict* is an organizational breakdown of the standard mechanisms of decision making. As used in social psychology, *conflict* is behavior that occurs when two or more parties are in disagreement. As used in personal psychology, *conflict* may refer to a person's internal struggle. As used in literature, *conflict* is whatever keeps a character from achieving a goal. As you can see, each academic discipline defines terms to meet its specific needs.

You must gain language skill in the academic field chosen and become familiar with the phrasing that identifies the potential subject of study. Once you are functionally skillful in the language used, you will be able to navigate for subject definition and topic identification. You can then translate the key ideas that provide definition for the subject of study. The next task is to translate your research interest into the academic language that will provide access to the scholarly conversation on the subject.

There are two jobs in Stage 3 of Figure 1.2: (1) becoming familiar with the academic terminology, and (2) gaining entry into the discourse about the intended subject of study. Before your first trip to the library, whether you are using the Internet (an electronic library) or a traditional brick-and-mortar library, stop for a second and review some important rules on library use. If you heed these rules, you will save time and produce better results.

Rule 1. Know Your Librarian

- The research librarian is a friend, a guide, and a coach. When using a library for the first time, consult first with the research librarian. Your consultation can be done at your university library or online, as available. Discuss the details of the research interest with the librarian. Be specific about your subject, your perspective, and your vantage point (that is, your academic field). Describe where you are in your literature review, and ask for tips and advice.

- Make sure that you have formed a positive relationship and can rely on the librarian as coach, mentor, and confidant.

Rule 2. Be Purposeful

- Have a clear purpose and plan when using the library. Wandering the stacks or exploring the subject catalog is entertaining, but it is not productive.
- Every time you enter the library, know what you are looking for and where to get it.
- Have a strategy for library work. Planning saves time. Know what you want to do before you take your first step. What types of information do you need, and where can those types be found? Are you scanning the subject catalogs to refine your topic? Are you consulting the specific subject dictionaries to define terms?
- Have a schedule of work and specific outcomes for the outing. Set goals and stick to them. Libraries present many temptations and distractions—a provocative title that catches the eye, a new book from a favorite author, an art collection on display. You must be disciplined. Be on time, schedule your breaks, and focus on the task at hand.
- Finally, before you leave the library, plan your next tasks. What other work needs to be done next? What is the time line? What new resources do you need? Address these questions as part of a debriefing before leaving the library. If you save debriefing for later, you invite ambiguity and misdirection.

Rule 3. Preparation Equals Efficiency

- Be prepared. Develop and organize your cataloging and documenting tools before the library visit.
- Cataloging consists of codifying the library materials you have accessed in such a way that you can easily refer back to them, and can properly identify them by the library system indexing for further reference. Cataloging tools range from simple three-by-five cards to research software tools such as *EndNote* or *Citation*.

- Documentation tools are stores of notable information. They can store notes about a subject, quotes and abstracts, further references to explore, subject maps, or a list of tasks to be completed next. Documentation tools contain library data collected for study. These tools, also, have various levels of sophistication, the simplest being a notebook or notepad. The more complex and integrated ones are software such as *EndNote, Citation, Microsoft OneNote,* or *ISO Researchsoft Reference Manager.*
- Take the time before you begin library work to build an organization system that fits your learning style and will aid you through the entire literature review. Organizing now will save much time and heartache later.

STAGE 4. VISIT THE LIBRARY

This exercise will guide you through the task of transforming the formal interest statement, developed in Exercise 1.1, into a preliminary topic of research. It has the following tasks:

Task 1. Make an appointment with the research librarian.

Task 2. Define the key terms of the interest statement.

Task 3. Translate the key terms and core ideas of the interest statement.

EXERCISE 1.6

Refining Your Research Topic Statement

Task 1. Make an appointment with the research librarian.

1. Explain your research project to the research librarian. Provide your interest statement and ask for review and advice. You may also want to confer with your research faculty adviser or other faculty member before this meeting for coaching on the formal research interest statement.

2. When meeting with the research librarian, review your interest statement. State the perspective and academic vantage point chosen for your interest. Seek advice on the clarity and specificity of

your work. If the librarian does not understand your interest as stated, go back to Exercise 1.5 and reframe your interest based on that information.

3. Ask the librarian to provide a survey of the library. Get the specifics of the inner workings of the reference section, stacks and holdings, periodicals, cataloging system, search capacities, and Internet access. Pay particular attention to the library's ability to address the academic field chosen for your study and your stated research interest. If you need more resources to complete your study, consult with the librarian.

4. Review the key terms and core ideas contained in your interest statement. Ask the librarian to direct you to the dictionaries, encyclopedias, handbooks, and other reference books that address these key terms and core ideas.

Task 2. Define the key terms of the interest statement.

1. Using your key terms, consult your chosen subject area dictionaries, encyclopedias, and handbooks. Find the technical definitions of your key terms.

2. Rewrite your interest statement using the technical terms of that academic field.

3. Review the reframed statement. Does it still express your intended interest? If it does not, rework and revise the study's focus and vantage point, or search the reference works further for other terminology to use until you are satisfied that the reframed statement expresses your research interest.

4. When the reframed statement works, go to Task 3.

Task 3. Translate the key terms and core ideas of the interest statement.

1. Taking your reframed interest statement, search the subject encyclopedias, handbooks, yearbooks, and other reference materials for topic areas that address the core ideas contained in your reframed interest. Rewrite as the topic of your study.

2. Document and catalog the results, noting prevalent authors and theory.

3. Begin to build subject and author maps for each of the core ideas in your interest statement.

4. Review your work. Check for accuracy and understanding.

TIPS

- Make sure your topic is specific.
- Focus the topic to ensure that it is clearly described and singularly defined.
- Select an academic vantage point.
- Avoid bias.
- Document, document, document.

SUMMARY

You now have the preliminary topic for study. You have successfully conducted personal introspection to uncover an interest, and you have defined that interest as a potential subject suitable for study. You are ready to a conduct a literature search. While the work seems linear, it is not. Notice that in Figure 1.2 everyday problems inform research interests. The opposite also holds true: research interests inform everyday problems. The thinking needed to unmask the specifics of these ideas is reciprocal in nature. The deep or fundamental understanding of one refines understanding the other. So it is with research interests and the academic discipline knowledge base. The more you learn about the topic through reading, the more refined that topic becomes. Refinement is an essential part of your subject exploration and topic definition.

This chapter begins with a general discussion of the method for transforming an everyday interest into a usable research topic. A model is presented that depicts the stages needed to reach this goal. This chapter then addresses selection of an initial interest for study, developing a usable research interest, and forming the research topic. The chapter ends with specific tasks and tips for accessing the literature and strategies for having a successful first library visit.

CHECKLIST	
Task	Completed
Define an area of interest.	☐
Define your key concepts and terms.	☐
Narrow the focus.	☐
Select a vantage point.	☐
Meet the librarian.	☐
Prepare documentation tools.	☐
Rewrite the interest statement as a topic statement using the correct technical terms.	☐
Begin your first library search.	☐

Search the Literature

Search Tasks and Tools

> *Veni, vidi, vici.*
> I came, I saw, I conquered.
>
> —*Julius Caesar*

The Literature Review Model

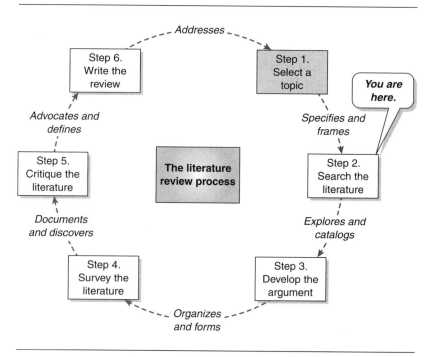

Y ou have successfully completed Step 1 of the literature review and are ready for Step 2, to review possible data for your topic. Some researchers make a serious error at this point. With paper and pencil or computer, they take the citations acquired from their subject and author query, go to the stacks or the Internet, grab books and journals, and begin writing furiously. They fall prey to the misguided notion that now is the time to write up the review of the literature. Remember, though: you cannot write about what you do not know. There are no shortcuts through this process. Before you can write the literature review you need to assemble the information on the topic and study it, thus gaining a thorough understanding of the subject matter. There is much examining, analyzing, and synthesizing to do before the formal writing can begin. By doing a quality search of the literature, which means reading and absorbing the information, you will be able to select the literature that needs reviewing, and then refine your topic based on the literature you select.

STAGE 1. DISCOVER THE LITERATURE TO REVIEW

At this point in the literature review, you must select the material you will review and the material you will not review. Several considerations decide what material is suitable to your particular literature search: Your main consideration must be gathering the information that addresses the key ideas contained in your topic statement. Other considerations might apply as well. For example, if your topic is time sensitive, you will need to look carefully at dates of publication before using information. A 1940s text is probably no help if your topic title begins, "Latest Theories on . . ." Perhaps, instead, your topic involves synthesizing the major works addressing a subject. If so, you will search for the important authors and theories about the topic, regardless of date. Your topic statement provides the direction and boundaries of your search. Using the topic statement as your pathfinder, continually ask yourself the following questions:

1. What is the subject of your inquiry?

2. What literature must you include that will tell you about the subject?

A second and equally important task should also take place now: you should refine your preliminary topic. The topic is fluid and subject to change early in the literature review. Your topic understanding is not yet influenced by knowledge of any literature. The data gathered while completing a search of the literature will impact your topic knowledge. This research of your topic interests will change as you gain a deeper understanding of the subject matter. The literature that you select in the search will qualify and refine your topic statement, thus causing your topic statement to narrow and become more concrete. As you research, reflect on how the topic is influenced and molded by the relevant literature you gather. For example, you may discover that your original topic is too broad and that it would be unrealistic to attempt covering all the information on the subject. Equally, you might find that your first topic choice is too narrow and that it fails to provide the substantial information necessary to answer your thesis question or statement.

Examine and reflect on the impact of the search data on your topic understanding. These deliberations will lead to creating a more concise topic statement. Be mindful and deliberate while conducting the search. Become aware of how the literature is influencing your topic interests. Keep these three questions in the forefront of your thinking when reflecting on your topic:

1. What is the literature telling you about your topic?

2. How is your understanding of your research topic changing?

3. What should your topic statement be now?

STAGE 2. CONDUCT A LITERATURE SEARCH

A methodical approach to searching the literature and reflective deliberation on the impact of the literature on your topic will provide a sound foundation for your literature review. You will know what you are looking for and why you are looking for it. How do you methodically search the literature?

The second stage of Step 2 requires collecting and selecting data. This stage has three separate tasks: previewing, selecting, and organizing (Figure 2.1). Begin the search by previewing the potential works for inclusion in the study. Then select the final works to

Figure 2.1   Literature Search Tasks and Tools

Search Task	Search Tools
Literature Preview	Scan
Content selection	Skim
Data organization	Map

include, deciding on their specific contribution to the research, their timeliness, and their accuracy. Finally, organize the specific ideas from each work selected for review.

Three tools will help you complete these tasks. These tools are your abilities to (1) scan the literature, (2) skim potential works for content, and (3) map the suitable works for inclusion in the study. While these are three separate techniques, you may use them in various ways depending on your ability and your topic selection.

Think of searching the literature as assembling a well-used jigsaw puzzle. There are always parts missing, and often pieces of other puzzles have become intermixed. Developing a strategy for assembling a jigsaw puzzle is simple. Find a table with room to spread out the puzzle. Ensure that you have enough room to sort pieces and to organize them. Make sure there is good lighting. Consider what the puzzle should look like when completed by looking at the picture on the box. Spread the puzzle pieces out on the table. Look for pieces that obviously do not belong, and set them aside. Look for the puzzle pieces that make up the outer edge. Assemble them, and sort the remaining pieces by like pattern. Look for matching color patterns and the specific shape of each piece. Finally, put the puzzle together one piece at a time.

Searching the literature is similar to assembling a jigsaw puzzle. Open the box, and spread the puzzle pieces on the table by consulting subject and author indices for potential texts and materials you might review. The key terms and core ideas of the preliminary topic statement define the search. They represent the boundaries of your research puzzle. Scan the library materials, collecting the pieces that are part of the research puzzle. Catalog the materials found to make them available for the next stage of the search—skimming.

Skimming resembles a first sorting of the jigsaw puzzle pieces. As with the jigsaw puzzle, data mined from the scan of the literature will be studied for usefulness. What should you include? What should you discard? Skim the materials collected in the scan to decide their appropriateness for inclusion in the study. Does this work address the topic? If so, how? The preliminary topic statement provides the frame for deciding what to include. Some puzzle pieces are not part of this jigsaw puzzle. Remove these first. Arrange those that remain into an orderly pattern. After deciding what works will be useful in the study, you then address the final task of the search, mapping.

As with the jigsaw puzzle, examine the material to decide its potential place in the literature review. How do these data explain a core idea? How do these data further define the key words of the topic statement? Organize the literature review puzzle by documenting the place each of the included works has in developing the topic statement. After completing the literature search, you amass the information for inclusion in the review. You first weed out data that do not directly address the topic, and then organize the selected works by key idea, noting the specific contribution that each work will make when explaining the topic. Remember the two questions that guide your literature search:

1. What is the subject of your inquiry?

2. What literature must you include that will tell you about the subject?

STAGE 3. SCAN THE LITERATURE

Begin the literature search by scanning the literature. A literature scan is a systematic canvassing of library and online catalogs, subject encyclopedias, periodical indexes, and abstracts. The scan's purpose is to identify potentially useful works, which could be books, articles, theses, dissertations, reports, and conference proceedings. When scanning, you should quickly examine each of the reference catalogs or guides, identifying the works you might want to include. Typically, you will engage in multiple scanning sessions, each designed to cover a particular view of the study. Each scan carefully identifies literature references based on their usefulness in building the topic's story. Design your scans to seek out various types of topic content, theoretical foundations and definitions, discussion and debate, current issues, field problems, and functional applications. Literature sources are usually categorized by these content types and are in chronological order of publication. You can place content types on a sequence based on specific content, publication type, and publication time frame (Figure 2.2).

As you can see, different reference types contain different categories of information. You would not look at trade magazines to search for the theoretical foundations of a topic, nor would you search definitive texts for recent issues or practices. Your strategy for each scanning session should consider the information category needed and the suitable research database that contains that literature type.

An academic literature review for practitioners most often demands that you seek both theoretical and field-based knowledge. Use current field-based literature to decide the issues, significance, and relevance of the study. The theoretical literature clearly defines the topic and provides the knowledge base for understanding the topic's depth and breadth. A search for the most recent data (see Figure 2.2) can help you gather information dealing with topic significance and relevance to the academic body of knowledge or professional practice. Specific databases contain different literature

Figure 2.2   Literature References

Recency	Years	Months	Weeks	Days	Current
←					→
Resource type	Books, monographs, and reference works	Journals and periodicals	Popular and trade magazines	Newspapers	Web sites and blogs
←					→
Content type	Theoretical foundations, definitions, research, key concepts, and constructs	Recent research, theoretical discussion, and debate	Current issues, debates, applications, practices, and field problems	Current issues, debates, and field problems	Up to date issues, debates, practices, and applications

types. Figure 2.3 provides a categorical listing of databases by literature type. For an up-to-date listing of databases that directly address the specific academic discipline of the study, confer with the research librarian, or consult the library's online database directory.

Begin the scan by doing a query of the reference databases that match the focus, vantage point, and content of the literature you are studying. For example, let's assume that you have identified your topic interest as theories of intelligence and that your selected vantage point is cognitive psychology. You might begin the search by querying online public access categories. This would provide a starting point, which might well lead to searches of each research database type as listed in Figure 2.3. Search directories are databases that use a query to obtain information. The most common query uses a Boolean logic to frame the database search. A **Boolean query** uses key words connected by the logical operators "and," "or," and "not" to define the search of the database. Using a combination of key words and one or more of the Boolean operators, you can focus the query and narrow the search to a specific area of interest.

Here is how it works. Select a key idea from your preliminary topic statement, and break it down by its key terms. Using the key terms as descriptors, combine the descriptors with the Boolean operators (and, or, not) to frame your search question. Use the operator "and" between two key terms to narrow the search selection. For example, say you are conducting a search about the key idea, "What is the nature of human intelligence?" Using three key terms—theories, human, and intelligence—a Boolean search might be as follows,

Figure 2.3   Reference Databases

Literature type	Books, subjects, authors	Refereed journals, subject periodicals	Theses and dissertations	Trade and popular magazines, newspapers	Web sites and blogs
Database	Library catalogs Online public assess catalogs	Library based and online subject indices and abstracts	Dissertation abstracts	Online indices Web query	Online search engines

"theories and human and intelligence." Notice that you can narrow the query by linking the two descriptors together to match the key idea. You can also narrow the search by author and subject: "Gardner and Wexler and Terman and intelligence." In this case, you are designing a query to find what these three theorists have to say about intelligence.

The Boolean operator "not" excludes terms from the search. Using the previous key idea, theories of intelligence, you query the database as follows: "theories and intelligence not emotional." This query will search for theories of intelligence and exclude any works that reference the word emotional in the text. When possible, avoid using the operator "not" since it tends to exclude documents you could actually use.

Using the Boolean operator "or" expands or broadens the query. The principal use here is to include similar ideas. For example, suppose you are exploring the key idea of the cultural bias of standardized tests. Frame the query in the following manner: "cultural bias and standardized tests or assessments or testing." Here you expand the query to include more descriptors that could well provide important banks of information about the key idea. Mix and match the Boolean operators to best fit the key idea of the search. You may need to use a trial- and- error method of framing the descriptors and operators into a statement in order to produce the needed result. Figure 2.4 summarizes the use of Boolean operators.

Figure 2.4   Boolean Operators

Operator	Topic search	Descriptor use
and	Narrows	Links descriptors
not	Excludes	Qualifies descriptors
or	Broadens	Adds descriptors

STAGE 4. USE THE INTERNET

You will probably be using the Internet for data gathering as part of your literature search. The Internet has quickly become a necessary storehouse for information and is in fact a virtual library. As with any library, the Internet supplies information from seemingly infinite sources. Be careful, though: Internet data sources vary in their credibility, accuracy, and soundness. Two major problems with the Internet are (1) it has no quality control, and (2) it has no librarian. In your university library, the librarian will help you find the data you need and will provide expertise in judging the quality of the material you seek. On the Internet, you must be your own librarian. You must judge data quality, authority, and applicability. Remember, anybody can put inaccurate information online. You don't want to quote from a paper written by a third-grade student, but such papers will be mixed in with scholarly works by experts in the field. Take extra pains to ensure that data you find on the Internet are high quality, authentic, and correctly cited.

We recommend that you use electronic databases provided through your academic institution. University libraries have developed a comprehensive collection of electronic databases to help you with your research. These databases have been checked by librarians and are at your disposal for doing research. Your library research staff can coach you through the use and applicability of the electronic references. These references can include online connectivity to virtual research librarians, access to the major journals and reports for your field of study, availability of virtual texts, connectivity to university library networks, and many other services. As you prepare to do your literature search, consult with your research librarian for coaching on the use of the electronic resources provided by your university. You should also check with a librarian on the best use of general Internet references.

One note of caution before leaving this topic: many of the journals provided through university electronic databases connect directly with your personal research databases (such as *EndNote, Citation,* and *Ref Works*). This means that you can cite a journal, transfer its abstract, and catalog its contents with one click of your mouse. The good news is that you can document and catalog this information quickly. The bad news is that little, if any, of this knowledge transfers to your consciousness. Make use of the great improvements electronic databases provide to the task of searching, but take the time to understand and internalize the meaning of your information as you collect your data.

STAGE 5. MANAGE YOUR DATA

Before scanning, you must address how you will catalog and document the scan information. Be aware that, without careful management, your data can overwhelm you. At this point in the literature search, you only need to log two types of information: bibliographic information and scan progress.

Bibliographic Documentation

For each entry, bibliographic documentation includes author, title, data, publisher, ISB number, pages referenced, and the call number. List each entry by idea or descriptor. You can do this simply by using the old standby of building a three-by-five card stack. However, we recommend that you use integrated cataloging and documentation software, such as *EndNote* or *Citation,* which is available at college bookstores and on the Internet. Use of software simplifies the process and allows you to integrate information as you go along. Basic bibliographic information serves as the reference point for succeeding search tasks. Documentation and cataloging are cumulative. With each new stage of the search you will have more information. Use a bibliographic entry card (Figure 2.5) to document your data.

Figure 2.5   Bibliographic Entry Card (front)

Author:	Key idea/descriptor
Year:	

> **Text**
> Title:
> Publisher:
> ISBN:
> Dewey decimal system number:
> Catalog call number:

> **Periodical**
> Journal:
> Volume:
> Issue:
> Pages:
> Catalog call number:

Employing the techniques and tools presented in this section, you can now perform the following:

1. Successfully develop a specific scanning strategy that connects the preliminary topic statement, its focus and vantage point to key ideas;
2. Frame key ideas as descriptors for the search;
3. Build Boolean frameworks to query the appropriate databases;
4. Develop cataloging tools to document the works you plan to review for potential inclusion in the study;
5. Define the sequence and purpose for each scan, and identify appropriate search databases and their accessibility.

Scan Progress

Keep a log that catalogs the material that your scanning has determined may be useful for inclusion in your research. Logging can be done in two ways: First, you can work directly from your Boolean query lists. As you scan, cross out items that will be excluded from your study. Use those items that remain from the list in the next stage of your research work. Date all of your work. This procedure ensures that you do not miss any potential resources. Second, following the same idea, complete the cataloging procedure using a database documentation program such as *EndNote*.

STAGE 6. SKIM THE LITERATURE

Now that you have scanned the literature to identify potential works for inclusion in your literature review, the next stage is to skim the identified works to decide what materials you will use. Skimming quickly identifies the important ideas contained in a text. While scanning identifies potential information to include in your study, skimming selects the best of all potential information. Here, you decide what to include and what to omit. Two standards guide you in conducting the literature skim.

1. Will this work be included or excluded from the study?

2. If included, what in this work is useful?

Use two techniques when skimming. First, examine and review the table of contents or index to locate specific material applicable to your topic. Second, do a quick read of those sections, chapters, or subchapters to decide whether (and if so, where) that information fits with the topic statement. Skimming identifies, organizes, and catalogs the specific material for review. Document the skimming results on the back of your bibliographic entry card. Figure 2.6 is an example of how this might look.

1. Begin skimming by reviewing the abstract or the text's introduction.

2. Does this material address the topic statement of the literature review? If so, how?

3. Continue by examining the table of contents of the text or major subject headings of a periodical. Note those chapters or sections that address the key terms or core ideas in the topic statement of the literature review.

Figure 2.6   Bibliographic Entry Card (back)

Author:	**Key idea/descriptor**
Selection review:	
Abstract:	
Notes:	

---

4. Document the results in the selection review section of the bibliographic entry card. Make sure that each entry documents the specific ideas and identifies the document, including page numbers, that you plan to use.

5. Once you have selected the specific areas of the text or periodical, do a quick read of that section to find the relevant information. Conduct a quick read by reading the first (introduction) and the last (conclusion) paragraphs of the section to identify the main ideas.

6. Skim read the section at three to four times your normal rate to quickly gather the main ideas.

7. Note the main ideas in the abstract section of the bibliographic entry card. Again, be sure to include page references for each major idea. Also, be sure to check all glossaries, appendixes, and other information in the end matter of the book. If there is a glossary, skim it for definitions connected to the topic's core ideas or key terms. Document these as well.

To continue the example from above, suppose the research topic is, "What is the nature of individual human intelligence?" The results of the literature scan identified several potential sources, which you have cataloged. You are ready to skim. One of the texts sited is *Intelligence Reframed*, by Howard Gardner. After reading the introduction, you decide that this text will make a major contribution to your literature review. In reviewing the table of contents, you find that Chapters 1 to 7 deal directly with your core idea, psychological theories of intelligences, so you note each chapter title and page number in the selection review section on the bibliographic entry card. You then read the opening and closing paragraphs, and skim the body of each chapter. You document the main ideas of each chapter in the abstract section of the bibliographic entry card. You also document, in the notes section of the bibliographic entry card, that Appendix D of the text contains the contact list for theorists in multiple intelligence theory. You then proceed to use this skimming technique for each of the texts selected.

STAGE 7. MAP YOUR MATERIALS

Now that you have scanned the literature and skimmed identified works to decide what materials you will use, you are ready to begin using mapping to form data patterns. Mapping is a technique for organizing the works that will be included in your literature review. Analyze each work for its contribution to the topic statement. Remember, the topic statement consists of core ideas and key terms. These core ideas and key terms are the descriptors on the bibliographic entry card. The content relevant to the descriptors should be noted and cataloged. In this phase of the search, you discover where each piece of the material gathered fits in with understanding the topic. Mapping allows you to organize the data collected into a pattern from which further analysis can emerge.

Use the descriptors created when you developed the preliminary topic statement as the central themes of your content maps. You might also create outlines that use the key terms and descriptors as major headings to map your data. Either of these methods can be effective for patterning your information.

Map and outline during the literature search to picture how material collected from the scan and skim addresses your topic statement; then develop content and author maps to pattern your information. Map the literature as follows:

1. Use your literature search key descriptors as central themes to create core idea maps. Map your data by each theme.

2. Compare your topic statement to your core maps to ensure the completeness of the information gathered by your scan and skim of the literature. If you find gaps or omissions, scan and skim the literature again.

3. Reorganize your data by author to document theory knowledge and citations. Expand your data detail when creating author maps.

4. Review your maps. Now that you have a general idea about the basic information addressing your topic, do you need to revise your topic interest? If so, rewrite your topic statement to reflect your new topic understanding.

Mapping by Core Idea

A core idea map isolates each of the core ideas of the preliminary topic as a central idea. These maps answer the question, "What is known about this subject?"

Review the model in Figure 2.7. Notice the core idea, or descriptor, is in the center and serves as the central idea or theme of the map. Each of the categories or parts that make up the core idea should be sketched as a subsidiary, or supporting, idea. These parts can be different theoretical positions, or they can be definitional or descriptive categories. Various arrangements are possible, such as

Figure 2.7   Core Idea Map

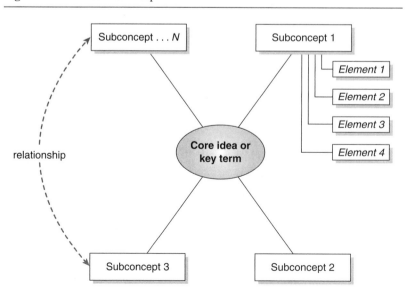

type, theme, or chronology, depending on what makes the most sense based on your particular research question. Break down each of the subsidiary ideas into individual categories, such as laws, theories, definitions, or examples. You may further break down individual parts as well. How you depict each of these maps will depend on the core idea and the parts that define it. The key to the successful development of a core idea map is the story it tells. As you develop the map, consider the following questions:

1. Is the depiction clear, inclusive, and comprehensive?

2. Does the map document the current state of knowledge about the core idea?

You should complete a core idea map for each of the ideas, key descriptors, or key terms outlined in your first subject map. One last word about core mapping: use this tool continually as you complete the remaining steps of the literature review. Core maps help navigate, survey, and analyze the literature. They serve as guideposts in refining the research topic. Finally, they are excellent reference tools for developing the composition outline of the literature review document.

Figure 2.8 is an example of a beginning core map on the history of the theory of human intelligence. The key descriptor, the main map topic, for this map is "The History of the Theory of Intelligence." Five themes were produced to address this descriptor, beginning with "Intelligence as an Abstraction." Notice that themes are arranged chronologically to show the evolution of intelligent thought. Each theme is further explained by subsidiary ideas, subtopics, which pattern the data you gathered by scanning and skimming. Each subtopic has author references to cross-reference the information.

Mapping by Author Contribution

The author map documents the literature review differently. It depicts the material assembled from the scan and skim of the literature from the vantage point of an authority. While the core idea map organized the material based on subject knowledge, the author map organizes the material by individual contributor. The core idea map answers the question, "What is known about this subject?" The author map responds to the question, "Who said it?" Figure 2.9 on page 52 shows an example of an author map.

Figure 2.8   Core Map Example: History of Intelligence

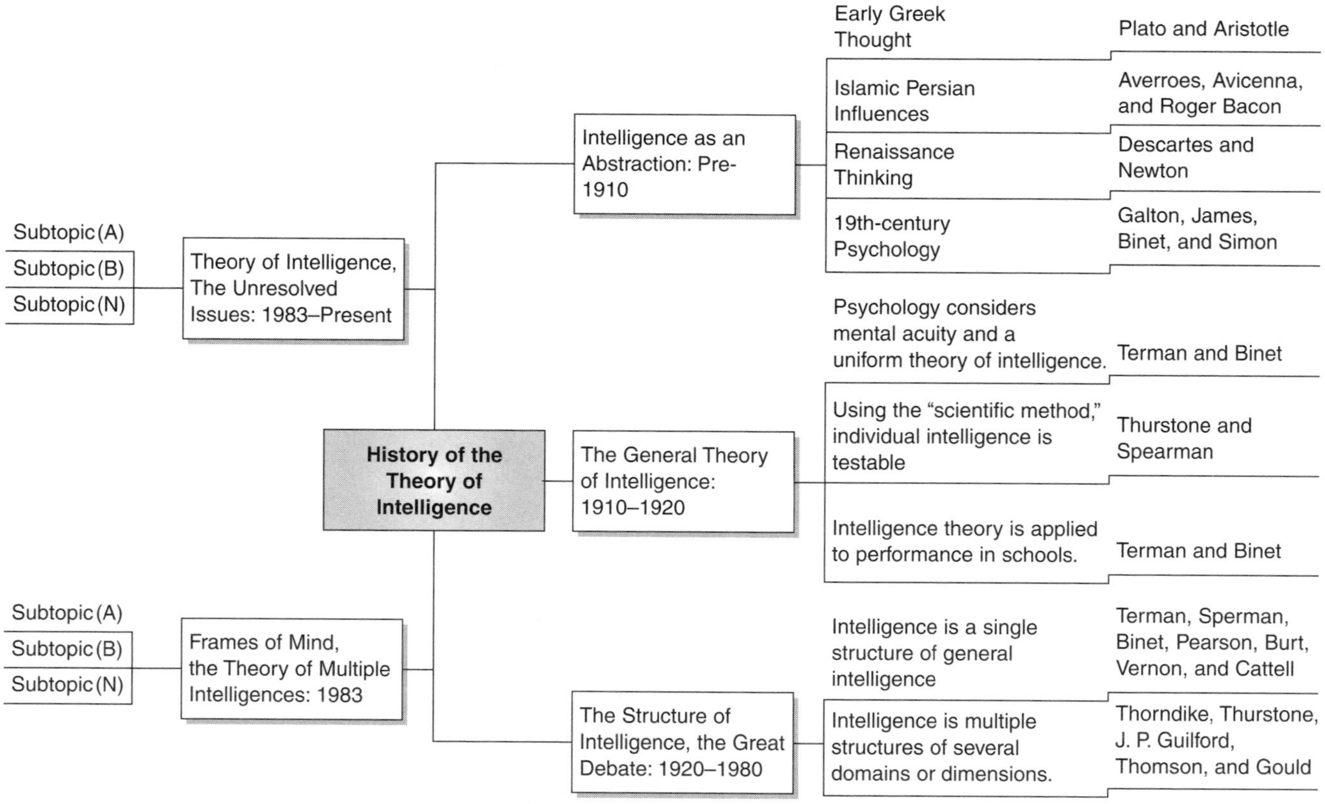

Plato and Aristotle

Averroes, Avicenna, and Roger Bacon

Descartes and Newton

Galton, James, Binet, and Simon

Early Greek Thought

Islamic Persian Influences

Renaissance Thinking

19th-century Psychology

Psychology considers mental acuity and a uniform theory of intelligence. — Terman and Binet

Using the "scientific method," individual intelligence is testable — Thurstone and Spearman

Intelligence theory is applied to performance in schools. — Terman and Binet

Intelligence is a single structure of general intelligence — Terman, Sperman, Binet, Pearson, Burt, Vernon, and Cattell

Intelligence is multiple structures of several domains or dimensions. — Thorndike, Thurstone, J. P. Guilford, Thomson, and Gould

Intelligence as an Abstraction: Pre-1910

The General Theory of Intelligence: 1910–1920

The Structure of Intelligence, the Great Debate: 1920–1980

History of the Theory of Intelligence

Theory of Intelligence, The Unresolved Issues: 1983–Present

Frames of Mind, the Theory of Multiple Intelligences: 1983

Subtopic (A)
Subtopic (B)
Subtopic (N)

Subtopic (A)
Subtopic (B)
Subtopic (N)

Figure 2.9   Author Map

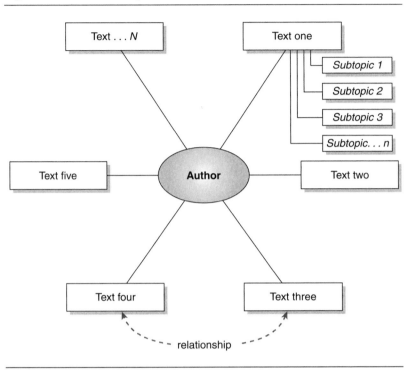

Author mapping provides the depth and reference specificity to support core idea mapping. When author mapping, you develop maps that depict the work of each author you cite in the literature review and cross-reference this information to a core idea map.

1. Note each specific text. Obtain this information from the author and selection review sections of the bibliographic entry card.

2. Record on your map the relevant ideas and details from the text, organizing them by content, theory explanation, or chapter headings and subheadings. You can find this information in the abstract and notes sections of the bibliographic entry card.

3. Record the relationships among the texts depicted on the author map. These connections compare theories, cross-reference subject

information, and develop chronological connections among texts. Place more information on these author maps, including page number references, notable quotes, and other authors or texts cited. As with the scanning and skimming techniques, adapt mapping skills and designs to your preferences and needs.

EXERCISE 2.2

Practicing Searching Skills

Practice what you have learned so far. Use the list you created in Exercise 2.1 to complete this exercise.

1. Select a method—three-by-five card, *Citation*, or *Endnotes*—for cataloging your data.

2. Enter the core ideas from your topic statement into your selected management tool.

3. Prepare your management tool for data entry.

4. Scan your references, and select one reference to work on.

5. Skim the selected reference for appropriate data to include in your review.

6. Enter the selected data into your management tool.

7. Develop a suitable core idea map.

8. Build a cross-referenced author map.

If you had difficulty completing this exercise, review this chapter. If you were able to complete this exercise successfully, continue entering other references into your management tool.

STAGE 8. REFINE YOUR TOPIC

Remember, the topic statement defines what is to be learned. It also forms the boundary of the study. This is an important notion. Not long ago we asked a colleague, a researcher from the University of

Chicago who holds a doctorate in his field, how he approached studying a topic. His answer surprised us: "For me, I spend less time thinking about what I am trying to study. Where I spend my time is in the hard thinking of what I am not going to study." The boundaries provided by the topic statement define the study from two perspectives: that which is to be studied and that which is not to be studied. This "hard thinking," deciding what is not to be studied, allows you to build a framed and focused topic of a study." How much is enough?" and "Do you have enough?" are the wrong questions to ask. The questions you should ask at this stage are the following:

1. Do you have a clear understanding of the core ideas in your topic statement?

2. Are these core ideas backed up adequately by your literature search?

3. Based on the literature search, how has your topic statement changed?

4. In reviewing your core idea and author maps, have you taken on too broad or too narrow a topic?

Completing a literature search gives you a great opportunity to refine the preliminary topic statement. You have done an in-depth study of your core ideas and key terms, and you know their main ideas. You may now revise the focus and vantage point taken in your topic statement for accuracy and clarity based on the information produced by the literature search (your scan and skim). After answering the four questions above, you may discover that your topic is too broad. The author maps contain hundreds of citations, and each individual core idea map could be a study in itself. What to do? The simple answer is to reframe the research topic statement by narrowing the focus. For example, your topic may be, "What are the negative connections that exist among members of a group?" When scanning the literature, you find an overwhelming amount of data addressing your topic, so you decide to narrow the focus. Your strongest interest is in the connections built among individuals in work groups. You refine your topic to now state, "What negative connections can exist in work-group dyads?"

Limiting the core ideas you plan to study and the specific theory areas you plan to include, or adopting a narrower point of view in the academic field are all ways of refining the vantage point. Limiting can also refine the study topic. You might further qualify your interest by selecting a specific vantage point. For example, your original study focus might have been group psychology and psychodynamics. You now refine your topic statement to ask, "What are the psychodynamics present in negative relationships of dyads in work groups?" By limiting the focus to a subset (dyads in work groups) of the larger category (groups), and by specifying a specific discipline to study (psychodynamics), your topic area attenuates to a workable dimension.

You can further define the subject demographically. You can delimit the topic statement by gender, age, experience, geographical location, ethnic background, or other qualification. In addition, you can further narrow the previous topic example by asking, "What are the psychodynamics present in negative relationships of dyads comprising adult males in work groups with a membership of fewer than fifteen?"

There are many ways to narrow your topic of study. Ask yourself the following when you are trying to narrow the topic:

1. What are you actually trying to study?

2. What are you *not* going to study?

As your guide to narrowing the topic, you should refer to the original interest statement you used to define your topic. Refer to your work in Exercise 1.6, Refining Your Topic Statement, to further edit your research topic statement.

STAGE 9. EXPAND YOUR TOPIC

You can also find yourself with the opposite problem: The results of your literature search may have produced scant information on the topic. In this case, you should review the key terms and core ideas developed in building your topic.

1. Have you defined your key terms and core ideas correctly?

2. Are there other definitions and academic vantage points that could produce better results?

3. Should the research become more inclusive by expanding either the focus or vantage point selected?

Examining the omissions and weaknesses found by the literature search is also a good way to expand the topic statement. When either narrowing or broadening the topic statement, you should keep in mind that quality is the critical standard of a research project. Narrowing or broadening the topic statement is not about how much work you need to do, but what work you must do to address the research interest.

TIPS

1. Be diligent. Slow down. Employing the many stages necessary for a high-quality literature search may seem time consuming. It is. However, the various tasks you perform correctly now will save time in the future. Careful, accurate research done once is much more efficient than hurried research that must repeated again and again.

2. Organize. Careful organization of information at the beginning will save you from the daunting task of trying to organize at the end when you have far too much material.

SUMMARY

You now have developmental and incremental plans for searching the literature. You know that a literature search is strategic data collection. It involves the three stages of previewing, selecting, and organizing literature for possible inclusion in the literature review. Three tools are available to help you in conducting the search. They are the techniques of scanning, skimming, and mapping.

- *Scanning* is an organized search of the library and online catalogs, subject encyclopedias, periodical indexes, and abstracts. The scan's purpose is to identify the works for possible inclusion in the study.
- *Skimming* is a rapid perusal of possible works to identify important ideas and their specific contribution to the research study, and to determine whether or not to use the work.
- *Mapping* is a technique that organizes the results of skimming to put the topic story together. Build core idea and author maps, and cross-reference them.

Use the information you now have to analyze the breadth and depth of your topic. After the search, you can select the works to include for review and, with careful reflection, can further define and refine the topic of study.

CHECKLIST	
Task	Completed
Previewing the Data	
1. Conduct scans of potential works by topic ideas and key terms.	☐
2. Conduct scans of potential works to build the case for study significance and relevance.	☐
Managing the Data	
1. Catalog bibliographic information.	☐
2. Create historical log of scan process.	☐
3. Create a database structure.	☐
Reviewing the Data	
1. Examine major parts of potential works for inclusion.	☐
2. Quick-read selected work for pertinent data.	☐
Mapping the Data	
1. Build initial core maps by key idea and key terms.	☐
2. Build maps by major contributing author.	☐
Refining Your Research Topic	
1. Refine topic statement for accuracy and clarity.	☐
2. Revise topic statement as necessary.	☐

Develop the Argument

Making the Case for the Literature Review

Quod erat demonstrandum
[That] which was to be demonstrated (QED)

The Literature Review Model

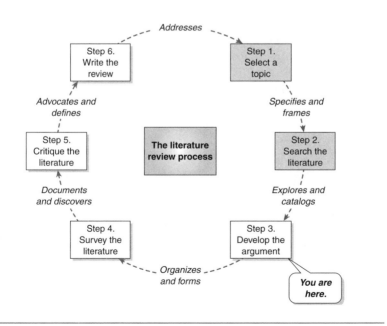

Y ou have now completed Steps 1 and 2 of the literature review process. You have spent time and effort collecting, cataloging, and documenting data. You probably think you are ready to plunge into the formal writing of the review, but you must resist this urge until you have read the next three chapters. Do not start a formal first draft of the literature review until you are confident that you will be able to state clearly the case for the thesis of your study. This does not mean that you should not take notes, draft outlines, or go back and review your work. In fact, you should be revising and rethinking at every stage of every step.

Formative work remains before you can begin to write a quality literature review. In order to discover your thesis, you must organize the data into categories and themes, and then you must analyze these findings to establish what is known about your topic of study. To perform these tasks successfully, you must build a case for what is known about the subject under study and determine how this knowledge addresses the research question.

STAGE 1. BUILD THE CASE FOR A LITERATURE REVIEW

Building a case means compiling and arranging sets of facts in a logical fashion that will prove the thesis you have made about the research topic. For example, if your thesis states that participatory leadership is the most effective style for twenty-first-century organizations, the data in your literature review must support and prove your conclusion. The following simple example demonstrates how to build the case for a literature review.

Picture an evening in early spring, when changing weather patterns are unpredictable. You are deciding what to wear to work tomorrow. Should you dress for rain? You look in your newspaper and see that their forecast is for rain. You check your barometer and find the pressure steadily falling. You look outside and see that cloud formations are building. You check online and see that the storms are predicted for the next few days. When considering all the information gathered, you conclude there is a high likelihood for rain tomorrow. You also decide that the available data indicate the rainstorm will probably hit during your morning commute. You apply the results of this research to your question, "What do I wear to work tomorrow?" and decide to wear a raincoat and take an umbrella.

Notice that two arguments were present in the example. The initial argument is, "Rain is likely." This first argument was made by using different sources to gather and combine information about weather conditions. The argument was constructed by analyzing the information from different sources and deciding that rain was imminent. Using this conclusion, it now becomes possible to address the question of whether to dress for rain. The second argument is, "I should dress for rain." This argument was built by interpreting the first argument, "Rain is likely." The results and conclusions of the first argument were applied as the basis for the second. These results reasoned that rain was approaching and that carrying a raincoat and an umbrella would be the most prudent course of action.

How does the example above apply to writing a literature review? In preparing a literature review you must also present similarly developed arguments to make the research case. An *argument* is the logical presentation of evidence that leads to and justifies a conclusion. The literature review uses two arguments to make its case. The first argument, called the **argument of discovery**, discusses and explains what is known about the subject in question. When building the argument of discovery, you develop findings that present the current state of knowledge about your research interest. For example, if your interest is to determine the ideal leadership style for organizations in the twenty-first century, then the findings discovered from the data documented in your literature survey must argue what is known about leadership styles.

The argument of discovery serves as the foundation for the second argument, called the **argument of advocacy**. The argument of advocacy analyzes and critiques the knowledge gained from the synthesis of the data produced by the discovery argument to answer the research question. The answer to this argument is the **thesis statement**.

Continuing with the leadership style example, let's say that your discovery argument produced findings that documented many leadership styles and their effective uses. Your advocacy argument must use these findings to determine which, if any, of these styles meets the needs of a twenty-first-century organization. You conclude, based on the evidence presented by your case, the participatory leadership style is best in the specific situation named. Your conclusion—"the participatory leadership style is the best fit for a twenty-first-century organization"—becomes your thesis statement. The two types of argument will be presented in detail in the chapters on Step 4 and Step 5. Before going further, we first need to examine the basic rules for making arguments and building cases.

STAGE 2. ARGUMENTS

When considering the word *argument*, you probably think of two people engaged in a dispute who disagree about an issue. Each is trying to overpower the other's belief, using arguments based on opinion, bias, belief, or emotions. These reasons, however, do not provide a legitimate foundation for a research argument. As seen in the introductory chapter, the use of the rational, persuasive argument is the stock-in-trade of the researcher. This type of argument uses reasoned discussion or debate to separate fact from fiction. Scholarly argumentation is not meant to overpower but rather to convince. The persuasive argument is logical. It presents a set of claims backed by sound reasons to support a conclusion. The reasons provided build on solid evidence.

The rules of the persuasive argument are simple: If valid reasons are presented that logically justify the conclusion, the argument is sound. If the reasons are not convincing or if the logic applied fails to support the conclusion, the conclusion is unsound. Here is a simple formula:

$$An\ argument = reason_a + reason_b + \ldots reason_n \therefore conclusion.$$

Apply this formula to the weather example presented earlier. Clouds are gathering ($reason_a$); the barometer is falling ($reason_b$); and rain is forecast ($reason_c$). Therefore it will probably rain during the morning commute. "It will rain on our commute" is the thesis of our argument (*conclusion*).

STAGE 3. EVALUATE THE
BASIC PARTS OF AN ARGUMENT

The following three questions provide a handy guide for checking the strength of an argument. Ask these questions whenever you are evaluating an argument:

1. What is the stated conclusion?

2. What are the reasons that support the conclusion?

3. Do the reasons argue for the conclusion? Do the reasons stated have convincing data to support them? Does the conclusion logically follow from those reasons?

EXERCISE 3.1

A Guided Practice

Review the following three arguments using the questions presented above. Write your answers to the three evaluating questions, and check your answers against ours, which follow each bulleted argument.

- Argument 1. Teamwork is necessary to get the job done. Jobs are completed only when teamwork is present. Teamwork and job completion go hand in hand. When groups act as teams, they succeed.

When you ask the first question, you can make conclusions. If you analyze Argument 1 closely, you find four conclusions: (1) teamwork is necessary, (2) completing jobs requires teamwork, (3) teamwork and job completion go hand in hand, and (4) groups acting as teams succeed. These four conclusions are redundant. When you ask the second and third questions, you find that no reasons are present to support the conclusion and that the reasons do not argue for the conclusion. Argument 1, then, is unsound.

- Argument 2. Teamwork is necessary to get the job done because individuals need to get their way to be productive. Individuals need to work independently of one another to produce good work. The central responsibility of a team is to allow all of its members their own space. Research suggests that individual identity is necessary for a group to remain cohesive. It further suggests that individual identity prevents groupthink and that individuality is the basis for creative work.

When you apply the three questions to Argument 2, you draw ambiguous conclusions. When you ask the first question, you cannot be sure whether the conclusion is, "Teamwork is necessary to get the job done," or if it is, "Individuals need to work independently of one another to produce good

(Continued)

(Continued)

work." When you ask the second question, you find some reasons to support the conclusion that independent action of a group member is essential to group productivity. No data are present, however, to support the reasoning. Finally, when you ask the third question, the reasons given do not support the conclusion. If "teamwork is necessary to get the job done" is the conclusion, the reasons support something different. Argument 2 is not sound.

- Argument 3. Teamwork is necessary for a long-term work group to be successful in the group task. We draw this conclusion based on the following research: "Study X found that when work groups engaged in group problem solving and collaboration, group communications and productivity increased. Study Y found that when groups engaged in productive interpersonal team skills and behaviors, group performance increased. Study Z measured team development based on individual member understanding of group mission, coordination, and unity. This study found that when these qualities were present in a positive sense, they were predictive of high group performance and productivity."

Argument 3 states a conclusion in the first sentence, thus answering Question 1. The support for this conclusion is research that is cited. When examining each of the studies, you find that they support the conclusion drawn, thus answering Question 2. When reviewing Question 3, we find that the reasons stated are logical and convincing. All the parts of an argument are in order here, and Argument 3 is sound.

Building an argument is simple. Before you arrive at a conclusion, though, be sure you can justify it.

A persuasive argument can come in many patterns and can employ sets of reasons formed into logical constructions of many sorts. The types of evidence and supporting data making up each reason can vary as well. However, regardless of the number of reasons presented, the evidence supplied, and the logical reasoning used, the case made must logically justify the conclusion reached. Figure 3.1 is a diagram that frames the **simple argument**.

Notice that Figure 3.1 contains the essential parts of a simple argument: the **claim**, the **evidence**, and the **warrant**. *Claims* are declarations of a proposed truth. *Evidence* is data that define and support

Figure 3.1   The Simple Argument

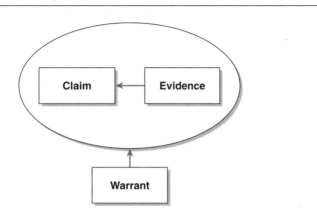

SOURCE: Adapted from Toulmin (1999).

the claim. The circle is the *warrant*: it represents the logical formation of the claims and evidence, and is the glue that holds claims and evidence together. The *warrant* employs a line of logic that justifies accepting the claim. The warrant is the "because" statement. Usually it is indirect (implied), although it can be direct. For example,

- "You should not cross the street."(Claim)
- "The signal light is red." (Evidence)
- The unstated rule implies that a red signal light means stop. (Warrant)

The simple argument represents the basic building block for making the research case.

Now that you have a general understanding of a simple argument, it is time to examine each part of the simple argument in depth. Claims, evidence, and warrants are the subjects for the rest of this chapter.

STAGE 4. CLAIMS

Claims

The claim is the argument's declaration or assertion. It drives the argument. In a persuasive argument, the claim is a declarative statement. A claim asserts a position, an idea that is put forth for consideration and acceptance. The claim made in our weather example was, "Dress for rain."

Chris Hart, in his text *Doing a Literature Review* (2001), suggests that claims are classified into five types: fact, worth, policy, concept, and interpretation.

Claims of Fact

Claims of fact are statements of proposed truth about a person, place, or thing. Claims of this type are the most often used when building the arguments for a literature review. The following are examples of claims of fact:

- California ranks forty-ninth among the fifty states in its funding for public education.
- Trans-fatty acids in foods are a major contributor to a high cholesterol count.

Claims of fact must be justified by evidence of truth.

Claims of Worth

Claims of worth propose judgments on the merit of an idea, course of action, behavior, or position over a competing set of alternatives. Evidence of acclamation—that is, evidence that has the strong agreement of others—proves these claims. The following are examples of claims of worth:

- Life in preindustrial society was morally superior to life in postindustrial society.
- Standardized testing is superior to course grades in determining student knowledge of a subject area.

Claims of Policy

Claims of policy are statements that set criteria or standards, directly expressing what one ought to do. Evidence of acclamation also supports these statements for taking a specific action or adopting a specific position. The following are examples of claims of policy:

- A policy that penalizes parents of truants by imposing monetary fines should be employed to lessen truancy rates in high schools.
- The best democracy is one that is decentralized and conducts its business locally whenever possible.

As with claims of worth, policy claims demand substantial evidence that demonstrate that the course promoted by the stated policy will produce the desired effect stated by the claim.

Claims of Concept

These claims either define or describe a proposition, idea, or phenomena. Concept claims are usually definitions justified by expert testimony. The following are examples of claims of concept:

- Emotional intelligence is an individual's interpersonal and intrapersonal competency in dealing effectively with others.
- "Groupthink" is a blind adherence to the force of will exercised by key members of the group, discounting any opportunity for consideration of dissenting opinion.

Claims of Interpretation

Interpretative claims provide a frame of reference for understanding an idea. Expert testimony, empirical research, statistical studies, or anecdotal case studies provide the evidence for interpretive claims. Researchers use claims of interpretation to build models, to synthesize data, and to organize factual claims. The following are examples of claims of interpretation:

- Keynesian theory suggests that government economic policy can effectively manage the national economy.
- American Lung Association research concludes that nonsmokers exposed to secondhand smoke at work are at increased risk for adverse health effects.

Figure 3.2 summarizes the types of claims, their use, and the suitable evidence for each.

A literature review seeks to answer a research question. That question seeks an answer of fact, judgment, standard, definition, or frame of reference. Figure 3.2 synthesizes these classifications. When beginning your literature review, analyze the type of claim needed to answer your research question. Knowing the type of claim needed signals the appropriate evidence and data needed to successfully make the claim.

Merely stating a claim does not automatically make it acceptable. The reader must have a reason to agree with the statement. Booth,

Figure 3.2   Categories of Claims and Their Uses

Claim category	Type	Argument use	Evidence
Fact	Statements of proposed truth about a person, place, or thing	Propose a claim of fact	Data verifying documentation
Worth	Statements of judgment of the merit of an idea, course of action, behavior, or position	Propose a course of action, behavior, or position	Supportive documentation by experts
Policy	Statements that set criteria or standards	Propose what one ought to do	Supportive documentation by experts or with anecdotal records
Concept	Statements that either define or describe a proposition, idea, or phenomenon	Propose definitions	Supportive documentation by experts
Interpretation	Statements that provide a frame of reference for understanding an idea	Propose a framework for combining concepts	Documentation by expert testimony, empirical research, statistical studies, or anecdotal case studies

SOURCE: Adapted from Toulmin (1999).

Columb, and Williams, in their text *The Craft of Research* (1995), state that all claim statements must meet four criteria to be acceptable: on point, strong, supportable, and understandable (Figure 3.3).

- An *on point* claim presents a proposed fact that relates directly to the argument.
- A *strong* claim provides a compelling reason to agree with the argument.
- A *supportable* claim is backed up by credible evidence.
- An *understandable* claim is presented clearly and precisely.

Figure 3.3   Criteria for an Acceptable Claim

1. On point	Relates directly to argument.
2. Strong	Gives a compelling reason.
3. Supportable	Evidence is available to justify the position.
4. Understandable	Specific. Clearly stated.

Here is a simple example of a claim that meets the four standards. You are taking a long trip by car, and you notice that you are getting low on gas. You ask yourself, "Should I fill the gas tank now or later?" and you claim, "I should stop at the next gas station and fill up."

This claim is *on point* because it addresses the question posed. It is *strong* because running out of gas would be a major impediment to the trip. The claim is *supportable* because your gas gauge reads nearly empty. Based on your experience, you know you do not have enough gas to reach your destination. Finally, the claim is understandable because it is presented clearly and precisely: You will fill the tank at the next gas station.

Here is an example of a claim that fails to meet the standards. You are taking a long trip by car, and you notice that you are getting low on gas. You ask yourself, "Should I fill the gas tank now or later?" and you claim, "I should have my oil changed." This claim would not be acceptable, because it is not on point (changing the oil fails to address the observation that you are running out of gas); it is not strong (because it does not provide a compelling argument for an oil change); it is not supportable (because the evidence suggests buying gas); and it is not understandable (because there is no clear relationship between the observation and the conclusion).

Here is a thesis that might appear in a literature review: "Student classroom success is directly related to positive classroom social interaction." What would an acceptable claim look like that addresses this thesis? For instance, you could make the following claim: "Individual student classroom success can be directly attributed to a positive interpersonal relationship with the teacher." To decide claim acceptability, apply the four points from Figure 3.3.

- Is this claim on point? Yes, since the claim states that a positive interpersonal relationship with the teacher promotes student achievement, it addresses one aspect of positive classroom social interaction.
- Is this claim strong? Yes, this standard has also been met because the claim provides confirmation of one critical part of classroom interaction, teacher-student relationships, and adds value to the case.
- Is this claim supportable? Yes, there are reasons here that support the claim.
- Finally, is it understandable? Assume that key terms and core ideas have been defined. The claim statement specifically defines actor (interpersonal relationship), action (causes), and result (student success). This idea can be clearly observed and analyzed, thus is understandable.

Evidence

The validity of a claim depends on the evidence you provide; evidence is the second leg of the simple argument (Figure 3.1). As claims drive the argument, so evidence propels the claim. *Evidence* is a set of data presented as the grounds for backing up the claim. You cannot simply assume a claim is true in an argument you make. By failing to provide supportive evidence, or by simply using personal opinion or belief as grounds, you fail to support your claim, and you fail to make a persuasive argument.

Data vs. Evidence

Data and evidence are not the same. *Data* are pieces of information. Information is value free and makes no judgment. It simply is. *Evidence* is data collected for a purpose, data with an agenda. Evidence is the basis for the proof of the claim.

To address your claim, you must search out relevant data, and you must compile it in such a manner that the position taken by your claim is supported. By selecting relevant data and compiling it to support your claim, you will have transformed data into evidence. Data alone do not signal a proof. However, data, selected and compiled as evidence, support a particular viewpoint: the claim. The quality and relevance of the data will control its value as evidence. You can see how data become evidence by using the rain example presented earlier in this chapter. The forecast is for rain; barometric pressure is steadily falling; cloud formations are building. When taken together, these data become the evidence that rain is likely.

Data Quality

Data quality refers to the strength and credibility of the data as good evidence. High-quality data build strong evidence.

- High-quality data are accurate. They present a true picture of the phenomenon being studied and are an unbiased report of an objective observation.
- High-quality data are precise. They present an exact measurement, description, or depiction of the phenomenon.
- High-quality data are authoritative. They are a product of sound research practice.

For example, you might cite the following datum as part of your research: "Study X, an explanatory case study, was conducted in a high-wealth school district with ninth-grade African American students from moderate to wealthy families. This study sought to explain the reasons for African American student success and failure in algebra classes. The study found that all students fail ninth-grade algebra at the same rate as their African American counterparts on the national level. When removing the variables of poverty, since the students came from a wealthy environment, it was found that positive interaction established between the algebra teacher and the student was the major factor accounting for student success. Students who did well cited their relationship with their teacher as a major reason for their success, while failing students cited the lack of this relationship as a major reason for their lack of success."

- Are the data accurate? You review the study and find that its methods for doing the research were sound. The study was conducted in a rigorous fashion. Its findings were validated. Based on this information, you are satisfied the data are accurate.
- Are the data precise? In reviewing the study, you find the interviews with teachers and students followed a strict protocol. The interview questions were structured and were based on well-defined characteristics. The interviews were conducted by trained interviewers, and the findings were validated by experts outside the study. The data are precise.
- Are the data authoritative? In reviewing the study's design, method, and procedures, you find the study followed the standards prescribed for case study research. Based on this assessment, you find the data to be authoritative.

Data Relevance

Data must also be relevant. To be relevant, data must meet two standards: Data must be appropriate, and data must be proximate.

Data are *appropriate* when they match the context of the claim. For example, if the claim is making a statement about secondary school teachers' opinions about standardized testing and the data report the opinions of elementary teachers, then the data are not a match. Elementary teachers are a different population of educators; therefore, their data do not necessarily represent the population addressed by the claim. The data are not relevant.

Data are *proximate* when they provide an accurate account of the phenomena observed. The vantage point or proximity of the observer controls data relevance. The *proximate standard* addresses the accuracy of the data observation. Was the account firsthand, or based on secondhand information? Were the data the result of primary research or secondary research that relied heavily on the research of others? Primary data from rigorous research have the best connectivity and are the most convincing.

For example, let's say that a claim makes the statement that more than seventy-five percent of elementary teachers find standardized testing to be of little or no help in planning their curriculum. This claim is based on the results of a national survey of elementary school superintendents (i.e., the data). Since the research did not directly seek the opinion of elementary schoolteachers, the data are not proximate. This research is weak because at best it is a secondhand account. We do not know whether its findings provide a true picture.

Qualifying the Claim

Building a strong claim requires that you present all sides of the debate. Rarely, if ever, is evidence for a claim one-sided. That is, in building evidence to support a claim, you will find data that support your claim and data that oppose your claim. Data that oppose the claim qualify it by either negating or narrowing the claim. Data that narrow the claim limit either the conditions of the claim or the scope of the claim.

Examples of negating data could look something like this: "The ABC study showed the target population rating in the seventy-sixth percentile in approval of the president's foreign policy. However, when the XYZ study administered a similar questionnaire under the same conditions to the same population, a significant difference was found. Approval had dropped to the fifty-second percentile." The data are contradictory, and their conclusions are in dispute. These studies negate each other.

Narrowing data qualify the claim's assertion. **Qualifiers** that limit conditions narrow the claim to specific circumstances. Claims can be narrowed by demographics, age, gender, ethnic background, or locale. Viewpoints such as personal experience, personal beliefs, or professional role can also narrow claims. Here is an example of narrowing data: "When given a survey, executive-level managers rated employment compensation as the chief determinant of their job satisfaction. When given the same survey, midlevel managers rated a collaborative work environment as the most significant determinant of job satisfaction." Here the claim asserting a specific reason for job satisfaction presents mixed results. The population surveyed expressed two preferences: compensation and collaborative work environment. The claim must be qualified to assert both viewpoints.

Limiting the scope of the claim narrows the claim's area of assertion. Usually, a global assertion claiming a single position of fact is not possible. Claims are always qualified by presenting all sides of the debate.

The literature review builds the case to advocate a thesis position. The case is built on claims supported by acceptable evidence, evidence using relevant and high-quality data. In almost every case, this evidence will present more than one side of the issue. The resulting claims made will set conditions, limits, or boundaries for the thesis, thus qualifying the thesis.

For example, we may state that, based on the data gathered, the evidence shows that student achievement is mainly the result of a positive interaction between students and teachers. However, we also find that factors such as economic background, student and family expectations, academic competency, and peer influences play significant roles in student success. These factors provide limits or boundaries for the thesis, and qualify the statement that student achievement is based on a positive interaction between the teacher and student.

Warrant

You cannot just present data without organizing it in some fashion so it can lead to the claim. Remember, data are evidence with a purpose: The purpose is to make and justify the claim. The *warrant* is the connection between the evidence and the conclusion. A *warrant* organizes evidence to draw a logical conclusion, thereby justifying the claim. The warrant is the third leg of the simple argument Figure 3.1).

The term warrant takes its definition from early medieval use. As used by monarchs, a king's warrant granted its holder permission to perform certain duties under the authority of the crown. The warrant was a letter of guarantee, a license, and a permit. It allowed the holder safe port and safe passage.

The warrant, as used in the persuasive argument, guarantees the argument safe passage to make its claim. The warrant is the logical license that ties the evidence to the claim, making the argument work. Warrants are logical ways of thinking and are seldom stated directly. Remember the example used earlier. Stop; the light is red. The evidence (the light is red) and claim (stop) are presented here, but the warrant is not. The implied warrant is that a red signal light means cross traffic has the right of way, thus justifying the claim to stop.

A warrant is created by presenting a logical pattern of evidence in a way that persuades the reader to agree with the conclusion made by the claim. Figure 3.4 illustrates the place of a warrant as the logical bridge in the simple argument.

Figure 3.4   The Simple Argument

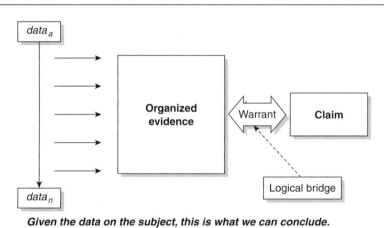

Given the data on the subject, this is what we can conclude.

You can discover the warrant of an argument by asking, "What is the reasoning used in this argument that allows you to accept the evidence presented as reasonable proof of the claim?"

For example, a claim is made stating that a well-balanced breakfast should be made available to children in elementary schools. The evidence for this claim comes from many research studies that show that children are more attentive and more mentally prepared to begin the school day when they have had a nutritional breakfast. What reasoning is used justify the claim? In this case, the reasoning used is that the evidence proves the claim beyond a reasonable doubt. If the evidence is sound and it overwhelmingly supports the claim, then you have to agree with the conclusion.

The reasoning behind warrants creates the logic of the argument. We will discuss these reasoning patterns and how they are used in the next chapter.

EXERCISE 3.2

Organizing the Formal Argument

Take time now to check your understanding of organizing a formal argument. We repeat Argument 3 in Exercise 3.1 for you to practice using this tool. Write your answers to the questions below, and check your answers to ours that follow.

1. What is the evidence given?

2. What is the stated claim?

3. Review the argument. What is the warrant? What is the reasoning behind the warrant?

Studies X, Y, and Z were used as reasons (evidence) to support the conclusion (claim), "Teamwork is necessary for a long-term work group to be successful in completing the group task." Here are our answers to the questions:

1. The evidence that supports the claim are the various studies cited.

2. The claim is, "Teamwork is necessary for a long-term workgroup to be successful in completing the group task."

3. The warrant is implied. The implication is that expert evidence is in agreement. Therefore, there is a logical bridge (the warrant) between the stated conclusion that teamwork is necessary for group productivity. The logic of the warrant implies that all the evidence, together, points to the same conclusion. Therefore, the conclusion must be correct.

STAGE 5. MULTIPLE CLAIMS ARGUMENTS

So far this chapter has dealt with the basics of argumentation using the simple argument. A *simple argument* is a single claim, its evidence, and its warrant. Most arguments are complex. **Complex arguments** are made up of multiple simple claims. These claims become the evidence to warrant the claim of the major argument. Build complex arguments as follows:

First, build multiple simple arguments using data as evidence to justify each claim.

Then, use the claims produced by these simple arguments to build the evidence necessary to justify the **major claim** of the complex argument.

Consider the following example: There are two simple claims: "Young women commit fewer classroom infractions than young men," and "Young women are more adaptable to social situations than are young men." These two claims lead to what we call a major claim: "Among all students, male and female, the best-behaved students are female." Notice that simple claims provide the foundation (evidence) for the complex argument and, when taken as fact, lead to a conclusion, the major claim. A model for the complex argument is seen in Figure 3.5.

As seen in the figure, simple claims provide the building blocks for the complex argument. Each simple claim becomes a **premise** of the complex argument. The premises act as data for the complex argument. A *premise* is a previous statement of fact or assertion (claim) that serves as the basis for a further argument. Premises are organized as the evidence for complex claims. The warrant used for justifying the complex argument can take many acceptable forms. The next two chapters will explain warrants in depth.

Figure 3.5   The Complex Argument

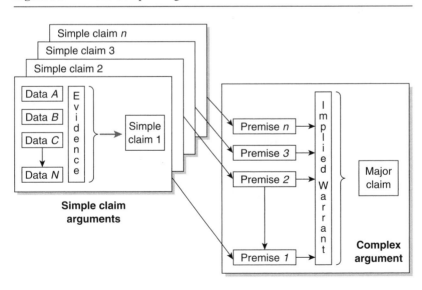

TIPS

- As you progress through your literature review, document the evidence for each claim. This is much easier than going back to search for lost evidence.
- Check Figure 3.3 often to ensure that your claim types match your argument use and your evidence.
- Be sure your claims are warranted.

SUMMARY

A successful literature review builds a well-argued case using logically framed arguments. Claims, evidence, and warrants make up a logical argument. A good argument proves claims. To do this, each claim must be built on credible evidence that validates its assertion. Relevant and credible data provide strong evidence.

Since data provide evidence to justify the claim's assertion, it is your obligation to present all sides of the question. Finally, the warrant supports the claim by using a logical justification to tie the evidence to that claim. Warrants use implied reasoning to justify the claim.

This chapter ends with a discussion on creating complex arguments. Simple claims are used as evidentiary building blocks to create complex arguments. These become the premises for justifying the central claim or thesis. Complex arguments are built in two stages: The first stage builds simple claims. The second stage organizes those claims into a body of premises that become the evidence for justifying the complex claim.

At this point you should have a fundamental understanding of the use of argumentation. How is it applied in a literature review? How do you, as the researcher, make use of arguments to survey and critique the literature? What are the strategies for successful argumentation of the case? These are the subjects of the next two chapters.

Below is a checklist to help you review the parts of your argument.

CHECKLIST	
Task	Completed

Checking your complex argument

1. Make a list of your preliminary conclusions.   ☐

2. List the premises that support each conclusion.   ☐

3. Do the premises justify (warrant) your conclusions?   ☐

Checking your simple argument

1. Make a list of your simple claims.   ☐

2. Check that each claim meets the criteria for acceptability.   ☐

3. List the evidence that supports each simple claim.   ☐

4. Check how your data are organized as evidence.   ☐

5. Are your data strong and credible? Check the standards.   ☐

6. Are your data relevant? Again, check the
    appropriate standards.   ☐

7. Properly qualify your data.   ☐

8. Warrant each simple argument.   ☐

Survey the Literature

Building the Argument of Discovery

Cui cerca, trova; cui secuta, vinci.
One who seeks, finds; one who perseveres, wins.

The Literature Review Model

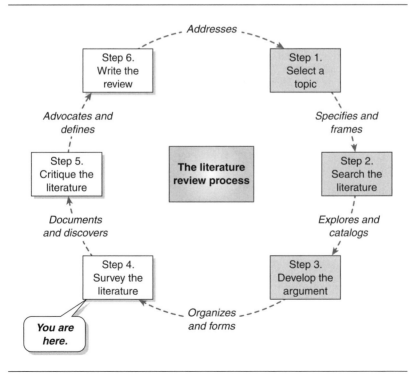

A good literature review must develop findings to provide a case that will prove the research thesis. In Chapter 3, you learned this case is made by presenting two arguments: the discovery argument and the advocacy argument. The *discovery argument* tells the story and answers the question, "What do we know about the subject of our study?" The *advocacy argument* answers the question, "Based on what we know, what conclusions can we draw about the research question?" The purpose of Step 4, the literature survey, is to develop the "What do we know" of the case. The literature critique is conducted after the literature survey and argues the "What can we determine" about the findings made by the literature survey. This chapter will discuss how the literature survey develops the discovery argument.

The *literature survey* gathers the prior knowledge about the subject of study. Surveying begins by examining the information gained from your literature search into findings. It concludes by building the findings into a storyline that describes what is known about the topic under study. Surveying is done in three stages (Figure 4.1):

Stage 1. Assemble the collected data.

Stage 2. Synthesize the information.

Stage 3. Analyze the patterns of the data.

STAGE 1. ASSEMBLE THE COLLECTED DATA

Assembling the Data

The literature survey begins with assembling the information. In Stage 1, assemble and evaluate the information gathered from the literature search. Assembling the data allows you to see all the puzzle pieces. As you look at the entire research puzzle, patterns appear, and organization can follow. Construct a central control document to assemble, organize, and analyze your data. You can design this document in varying styles and formats, depending on your individual need. Figure 4.2 on page 84 is an example.

Figure 4.1   Literature Survey Process

Survey Stages	Tasks
Stage 1. Assemble the collected data.	Catalog and document major works of recognized importance—journals, texts, etc. Build lists of authors. Catalog citations. Review the quality and strength of the information. Create survey tally matrix. Document core ideas.
	↓
	Arrange and categorize major works into categories—by author, key descriptor and theme, chronology, theory, etc.
	↓
Stage 2. Synthesize the information.	Organize core maps and outlines according to theme patterns.
	↓
	Expand tentative author maps, theory maps, bibliographic entry card abstracts, and notes to build prevailing theories, principles, etc. Build simple claims.
	↓
	Examine core maps and tally matrices to formulate an argument scheme and reasoning pattern to determine "what is known" about the research topic.
	↓
Stage 3. Analyze the patterns of the data.	Create a storyline. Mind map and outline discovery argument. Build complex arguments and major claims.
	↓
	Compose an exploratory document on the current state of knowledge about the research subject. "Tell the story."

Recording the Data

At the end of the literature search, you built subject maps, core maps, and bibliographic entry cards. Using those data, you can now assemble this information in a central document for review and organization. Begin the assembly task by recording the data compiled from the bibliographic entry cards onto the tally matrix. Record relevant data for each entry in Columns 1, 2, and 3. Now conduct a quality review of the data gathered. Record your assessment of quality

Figure 4.2 Literature Survey Tally Matrix

	Stage 1. Assemble the collected data.				Stage 2. Synthesize the information.				Stage 3. Analyze the patterns of the data.		
	Key concept or descriptor (1)	*Citation or reference (2)*	*Main ideas (3)*	*Data quality (4)*	*Evidence categories (5)*	*Warrant scheme and simple arguments (6)*	*Simple claim statement (7)*	*Claim acceptability (8)*	*Simple claim statement (premises) (9)*	*Warrant scheme and complex argument (10)*	*Complex claim statement (11)*
	Taken from maps and bibliographic entry card	Taken from maps and bibliographic entry card	Taken from maps and bibliographic entry card	Do data meet quality standards? (yes or no)	Data entry placement into a body of evidence	Warrant scheme used for this evidence group	Data entry is evidence for this claim	Does claim meet acceptability standards? (yes or no)	Simple claim placement as an evidence statement for the major claim	Warrant scheme used to justify the complex argument	The thesis for the discovery argument
Author Text Periodical (A)											
Author Text Periodical (B)											
Author Text Periodical (C)											
Author Text Periodical (n)											

in Column 4. As needed, review Chapter 3 for the specific standards used to assess data quality and relevance.

While you might want to transcribe the entirety of the material to the tally matrix, it would be cumbersome to do so. Here are three alternatives to total transcription of the data.

1. You can use simple coding for cross-referencing the source documents and the central documents. The simplest method is to assign an alphabetic code by author or text. You can use abbreviations or key words to record the core ideas in the selection review and abstract sections. The important notion here is that key ideas be decipherable on the tally matrix and that tallying does not become an impossible task. When using a coding scheme, ensure that all information can easily refer back to the original source.

2. You can use reporting found in integrated software programs such as *Citation* or *EndNote*. Each of these programs can query, search, and report while generating tally documents. When using these electronic programs, you can edit and tailor the electronic reports to include the parts of the tally matrix not addressed by the software. Once you have completed recording all the references in the first four columns of the tally matrix, you can begin analyzing the data, building evidence, and developing claims.

3. You can use butcher paper or large sticky notes to assemble the data using storyboard techniques. When using this alternative, you can directly transcribe the data in longhand or cut and paste data to the storyboard.

You can also use a combination of these options to suit your individual skills and preferences.

STAGE 2. SYNTHESIZE THE INFORMATION

Synthesizing the Information and Building Evidence

In Stage 1 of the literature survey, you assembled the data collected by the literature search. Now, in Stage 2, you will pattern the data to form a body of evidence to create simple claims. To start, examine the entries made on the tally matrix (Columns 1–3) to determine how the data fit together. Remember, *evidence* is data with a purpose. How are the data combining to tell the story? Examine the data contained on the tally matrix by key descriptor, core idea, or author to develop a picture of the data entries as evidence (Figure 4.3).

Use your core idea and author maps to assist you in building the data entry picture. Perhaps you can group the entries best by a time period. If so, organize your matrix data chronologically. Alternatively, the evidence might best be organized by theme. If so, combine bodies of evidence thematically for purposes of comparison or modeling. Finally, you might want to group data into an evidence pattern by various authors to discover trends or characteristics of a topic.

There are many ways to organize data into evidence. Your decision about how to organize data will depend on the nature of your research problem. Again, you need not limit yourself to the use of one evidence pattern. Trying different groupings allows you to examine how best to produce the body of evidence. Perhaps a combination of data groupings is the most suitable method for patterning your data.

As evidence patterns form, document them. Develop a coding scheme to catalog your evidence. The coding scheme should employ key words or alphanumeric symbols as codes for organizing the evidence. Use a code sheet to list each of the code entries with a short statement describing its identified evidence group. Enter the codes for evidence categories in Column 5 of the tally matrix. The code sheet is an indispensable reference for further work.

Refer back to Figure 2.8 for an example of how coding works. The key descriptor, "History of the Theory of Intelligence," is in five major parts. A chronological scheme organizes the data. Each of the five major parts is further divided into subsections. For purposes of demonstration, let us develop codes for the first major part entitled, "Intelligence as an Abstraction (Pre–1910)." Use "pre–1910" as a code for the major part. Use "EGT" as a code to catalog data belonging to the "Early Greek Thought" subcategory, and "IPI" as code to catalog data belonging to "Islamic Persian Influences." You can develop the initialing for the contents of the entire core map. Your code sheet would note the titles of the major parts and subcategories and the matching abbreviations, which are now available for future reference. Continue this process until you have completed coding and organizing all your data.

At this point of the survey, you have organized data into patterns of evidence, which you now need to warrant. Evidence must be

Figure 4.3 Literature Survey Tally Matrix: Stage 1

	Key concept or descriptor (1)	Citation or reference (2)	Main ideas (3)	Data quality (4)
Stage 1. Assemble the collected data.				
	Taken from maps and bibliographic entry card	Taken from maps and bibliographic entry card	Taken from maps and bibliographic entry card	Do data meet quality standards? (yes or no)
Author Text Periodical (A)				
Author Text Periodical (B)				
Author Text Periodical (C)				
Author Text Periodical (n)				

formed using an acceptable reasoning pattern to create a warranting scheme that justifies the simple claim. Your key to success at this critical stage is your ability to see that reasoning pattern.

Reasoning Patterns

Whether unraveling the plot of a good detective novel or assembling a jigsaw puzzle, the reasoning is the same as you are using in creating the literature review. There are basic patterns in any of these scenarios, and they can be used to organize research evidence and claims to form the argument of discovery. Alec Fisher, in his texts *The Logic of Real Arguments* (2003) and *Critical Thinking: An Introduction* (2004), classifies the basic reasoning patterns into four types: one-on-one reasoning, side-by-side reasoning, chain reasoning, and joint reasoning.

These patterns of reasoning move from the simple to the complex. Each pattern serves as a potential organizer for the logical patterning of the connections between data groupings. These patterns are the warranting schemes for connecting evidence to claims. A discussion of each of these reasoning patterns and mapping schemes is in order.

- One-on-one reasoning. The most elementary reasoning pattern is a simple connection between reasoning and a conclusion. Its diagram is

$$R \therefore C.$$

In this simple pattern, one reason (*R*) is enough to justify the conclusion (*C*) (as shown in Figure 4.4). This one-on-one reasoning can be proven as true or false. For example, "The noon bell has rung. Therefore, it must be lunchtime."

Here you have one datum that convincingly leads to the claim. The map (Figure 4.4) depicts simple cause and effect, or one datum to justify the claim.

Figure 4.4   The One-on-One Map

- Side-by-side reasoning. A side-by-side reasoning pattern cites several data entries, all of which offer the same reason to justify the conclusion. Here is a diagram of the side-by-side pattern:

$$R_1, R_2, R_3, R_4 \ldots R_n \therefore C.$$

This is the pattern used as an example of warranting reasoning used in Chapter 3 and is the scheme often used by social science researchers in arguing claims for a literature review. This pattern typically uses several authors or theorists in support of the claim, like this: Expert opinions, research studies, statistics, expert testimony, and other data all point to the same conclusion. An evidentiary pattern is built as one would build a stone wall. The result, as shown in Figure 4.5, is a collection of overwhelming evidence leading to a conclusion.

You can use convergent mapping to present a claim. Such maps are cumulative in their logic, which is an apt pattern to use when you find several data entries that independently confirm the conclusion. This is a justified claim because of the

Figure 4.5   Convergent Mapping

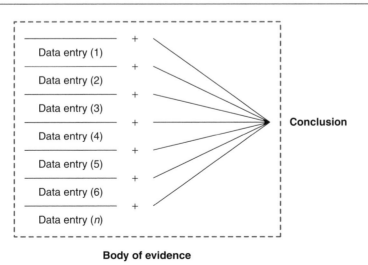

Body of evidence

sheer number of confirming entries. For example, the evening news forecasts rain; the radio forecaster says it will rain; the Internet forecast predicts rain; therefore, it will probably rain.

- Chain reasoning. Chain reasoning is another pattern widely used by researchers in building an argument. Serial in nature, it begins by citing one or more reasons that justify a conclusion. It uses a one-on-one reasoning pattern as its foundation. The conclusion of the first pattern then becomes the evidence for the second conclusion. This line of logic continues until the final conclusion has been justified. Here is the diagram for a chain reasoning pattern:

$$(R_1 \therefore C_1) + (C_1 \therefore C_2) + (C_2 \therefore C_3) + \ldots (C_{n-1}) \therefore C_n.$$

Notice that this pattern forms as if you were making a daisy chain (Figure 4.6). Each link of the chain becomes the premise for arguing the next conclusion. The thought pattern is, "If this, then that; because of *a,* then *b;* because of *b,* then *c.*" Each conclusion thus becomes the reason that builds the next conclusion, continuing the reasoning pattern.

You can use chain reasoning to link or develop connections among reasons to form an overall conclusion. In chain

Figure 4.6   Chain Reasoning

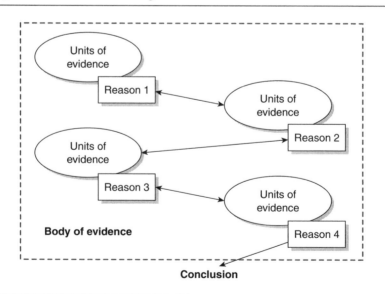

reasoning, the claim of one set of data will have a bearing on the claim of another set of data. These linkages can be a qualification of one claim on another, a causal connection between claims, an association between claims, or an evolutionary connection of one claim to the next. This mapping scheme is useful in tracking chronological data entries and theory development. For example, "Car engines burn less gas when they work at lower speeds, so lower speeds mean less gas consumption; less gas consumption means fewer toxic fuel emissions; fewer toxic fuel emissions mean less air pollution; therefore, reducing the speed limit means less air pollution."

- Joint reasoning. Joint reasoning provides a fourth pattern for organizing data to justify a conclusion. In this case, the reasons stipulated cannot stand on their own, but, when taken together, provide the necessary reasoning to justify the conclusion. A diagram of a joint reasoning pattern is

$$(R_1 + R_2) \therefore C.$$

Notice here that neither R_1 nor R_2 alone provides enough justification to form the conclusion. However, R_1 and R_2 together allow you to logically draw a conclusion. This thought pattern is demonstrated in the following manner: "If X exists, and Y exists, then Z." If one of the partial reasons (X or Y) is not present, then you have no justified conclusion. Review the following example: "When the temperature falls below freezing and enough moisture is present, it will probably snow."

Use joint reasoning when you find that data entries build a theory or a position (Figure 4.7). The logic for this map is additive in nature. Notice that the individual datum

Figure 4.7   Joint Reasoning

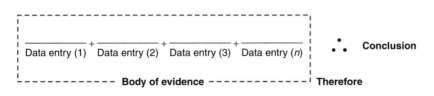

represented by each entry does not justify the conclusion on its own merit. Only when the entries combine can the conclusion be made. The data are parts that together make up a theory or position.

Integrating the Information and Building Claims

Applying the previously discussed reasoning patterns as warranting schemes to your evidence groups will produce justified claims. To create the simple claim, transcribe your work on the tally matrix section as shown in Figure 4.8.

1. Begin by reviewing each data grouping by evidence category. Examine how the data fit together; then apply the correct reasoning pattern to each evidence group.

2. Record the reasoning pattern (warranting scheme) for each data group in Column 6 of your tally matrix.

3. Find the conclusion deduced (the **deduction**) from each of your organized patterns of evidence. Write it as a declarative sentence. This is your claim.

4. In Column 7, write the claim or assertion created by the evidence.

5. After completing your claim statements, evaluate the acceptability of each claim. Is it on point, powerful, debatable, and clearly stated? (Refer to the section Acceptability of Claims in Chapter 3.)

6. Record your claim evaluation in Column 8.

EXERCISE 4.1

Practice in Organizing Data and Building Claims

Use your research to practice organizing data and building claims. Select a key descriptor from your work. Create a shortened version of Figure 4.2 (the Literature Survey Tally Matrix) and complete Columns 1–4 using the data you have collected. For Columns 5–8, follow the tasks listed in Stage 2.

Figure 4.8   Literature Survey Tally Matrix: Stage 2

	Stage 2. Synthesize the information.			
	Evidence categories (5)	Warrant scheme and simple arguments (6)	Simple claim statement (7)	Claim acceptability (8)
	Data entry placement into a body of evidence	Warrant scheme used for this evidence group	Data entry is evidence for this claim	Does claim meet acceptability standards? (yes or no)
Author Text Periodical (A)				
Author Text Periodical (B)				
Author Text Periodical (C)				
Author Text Periodical (n)				

The preliminary work of building simple arguments is done. You have organized and gathered your information into strong bodies of evidence that produced acceptable claims. Now you need to find the connections that exist among the simple claims to build the complex argument for "what is known" about your research subject.

STAGE 3. ANALYZE THE PATTERNS OF THE DATA

To explain what is known about the subject, build the discovery argument. Make this argument by arranging the simple claims you developed in Column 7 of the Tally Matrix from Stage 2 into a complex argument. This task demands analysis, which is the purpose of Stage 3 of the literature survey.

Analysis begins by reviewing the simple claims created in Stage 2 to discover their logical connection pattern. This pattern will present the claims in a reasoned order—a warrant scheme. The simple claims now become premises for the complex argument.

Critically analyze the evidence and claims by asking the questions, "What do these data say?" "What's the story?" "How do the facts fit together?" As the chief detective in a good mystery novel, you must unravel the plot by examining the evidence to decide, "What happened?" "Who did it?" Analysis of the evidence by combining the claims in some significant way enables you to compose the story, to make the argument. How does the detective—you, in this case—logically develop evidence and claims into a well-argued story? Using the argument schemes as guides, you can either outline or map the argument. The outline enables you to compose an exploratory draft as the first effort to tell the story of what is known about the subject of the research. If you are new to exploratory writing or if you need to review it, read the explanation and exercise in Chapter 6, found under the section "Exploratory Writing: Creating Writing Readiness."

Complex Reasoning

Complex reasoning is often used by researchers to organize claims into complex arguments. This warranting scheme employs two or more of the four basic reasoning patterns to build the central argument: one-on-one reasoning, side-by-side reasoning, chain reasoning, and joint reasoning. A complex pattern combines the basic patterns as building blocks to organize the premises that form the discovery argument. The basics for the complex argument are in Chapter 4, "Multiple Claims Arguments." Review Figure 3.5 as a reminder. Two regularly used complex warranting schemes that build arguments of discovery are divergent reasoning and comparative reasoning.

Divergent Reasoning

This pattern depicts an academic debate. Divergent reasoning is an offshoot of the basic side-by-side reasoning pattern:

$$R_1, R_2, R_3, R_4 \ldots R_n \therefore C_A \text{ versus } R_1, R_2, R_3, R_4 \ldots R_n \therefore C_B.$$

Cite several expert opinions, research studies, statistics, expert testimony, and other data in a way that builds an evidentiary pattern for one side of the question, then cite another set of data to show the opposing view.

Divergent Mapping

The pattern in Figure 4.9 maps opposing viewpoints. Use this pattern to depict any authors' positions, research findings, or theories found in the evidentiary data that are in direct contradiction. By

Figure 4.9   Divergent Mapping

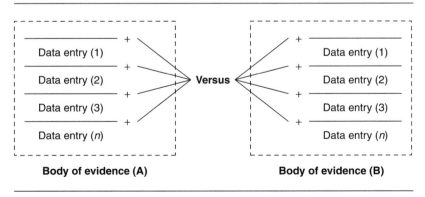

Body of evidence (A)   Body of evidence (B)

mapping the opposing data, you can graph the vantage point and the focus of each position to discover the strong and weak points for each side of the debate.

Comparative Reasoning

The comparative reasoning scheme shows connections between groups of data. Here you are examining likenesses and differences in each group by comparing and contrasting the evidence and claims associated with each position. This complex reasoning pattern symbolically looks like the following formula:

$$R_1, R_2, R_3, R_4 \ldots R_n \therefore C_A \wedge R_1, R_2, R_3, R_4 \ldots R_n \therefore C_B.$$

As with side-by-side reasoning, you cite expert opinions, research studies, statistics, expert testimony, and other data to build an evidentiary pattern for the first claim group (A). The set of data from the next claim group (B) is also presented. Look at the differences and likenesses between the data presented, and compare and contrast the two side-by-side arguments. You can graphically represent this reasoning by using a Venn diagram (Figure 4.10).

Figure 4.10   Venn Diagramming, Comparative Mapping

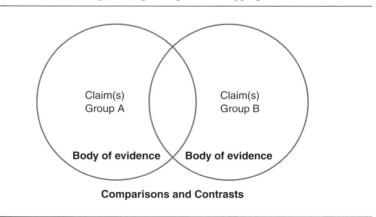

Comparisons and Contrasts

Venn diagrams map the connections between two or more data groups. They are commonly used when charting the relationships between theoretical data, opposing positions, two populations, or alternative methods. Each circle in the Venn diagram represents one body of evidence. Once you have described each claim, you can easily show the commonalities of the combined claims by noting those parts of each claim that fall inside the circles' intersection. To see the differences, note those parts that fall outside the intersection.

Building the Discovery Argument: An Example

The following is an example of the use of complex reasoning to form an argument about a topic of study. Suppose the subject of study is "The Definition of Human Intelligence in the Twentieth Century: A Cognitive Perspective." The literature survey documents the seminal works on the subject. After you complete the appraisal tasks in surveying the literature, three themes emerge:

1. Human intelligence consists of a single structure, as opposed to the position that human intelligence consists of multiple structures of several domains or dimensions.

2. Human intelligence can be accurately measured, as opposed to the position that human intelligence cannot be accurately measured.

3. Human intelligence is inherited and static, as opposed to the position that human intelligence is changeable and developmental.

Perhaps you mapped the first theme, single versus multiple intelligences, as shown in Figure 4.11. This researcher selected divergent mapping as the scheme to organize the data. As you can see in the figure, multiple simple arguments make up the body of evidence for both theories of intelligence. First, you must develop each of the simple arguments of the scheme. Notice that in this case each simple argument depends on the theory of a specific author.

To continue the example, we will map and pattern a simple argument from each competing theory: Spearman's theory for the General

Figure 4.11   Theme One: The Nature of Intelligence

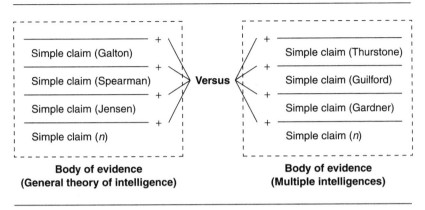

Theory of Intelligence and Gardner's Theory for Multiple Intelligences. A simple map can chart Spearman's theory of intelligence, and a one-on-one reasoning pattern explains his theory:

$$R \therefore C$$

Positive Manifold = Intelligence Level.

Spearman declared that one single general cause governs the intelligence of an individual. He called that general cause a *positive manifold* (which he defines in his work).

Chain reasoning diagrams this theory as follows:

$$(R_1 \therefore C_1) + (C_1 \therefore C_2).$$

In narrative form, you can express this theory as follows: If certain parts of the brain can map with certain cognitive functioning, then that cognitive role can be isolated as one of the multiple intelligences. Certain parts of the brain distinctively map with certain cognitive functioning; therefore, there are multiple intelligences. Gardner has identified eight specific intelligences that identify with unique human cognitive functions of intelligence. He has determined each of these intelligences based on the chain reasoning used in Figure 4.11. Assume that the theory offered by each of the authors was reasoned as a simple argument. You must now develop a reasoning pattern for the complex argument.

You continue using divergent mapping as the overall scheme for the argument. Side-by-side reasoning builds the body of evidence for both the General Theory of Intelligence and the Theory of Multiple Intelligences. It is diagrammed as follows:

$$R_1, R_2, R_3, R_4 \ldots R_n \therefore C_A \text{ versus } R_1, R_2, R_3, R_4 \ldots R_n \therefore C_B.$$

Using the additive roles of side-by-side reasoning, you compile each of the simple arguments as separate reasons for justifying the conclusion. Combining the arguments by Spearman, Galton, Jensen, and others produces the body of evidence that proposed the claim for the General Theory of Intelligence. Compiling the work of Guilford, Thurston, Gardner, and others in the same fashion produces the evidence for the Theory of Multiple Intelligences.

Reasoning patterns are invaluable aids in developing arguments for a literature survey. First, simple reasoning patterns are applied to form simple arguments and claims. These claims now become premises and are organized as evidence for the complex argument. Complex reasoning patterns are used again to determine the warranting scheme that justifies the major claim of the complex argument. To build the complex reasoning for the discovery argument, use Stage 3 of the tally matrix (Figure 4.12).

Mapping the Argument of Discovery

To begin the analysis, review the claims posted in Column 8. Reorganize these claims using complex reasoning patterns. Regroup the corresponding arguments for each claim by these patterns. Now record the reordered claims, stating them as premises in Column 9. Analyze the premises made in Column 9; determine the reasoning pattern that will serve as the warranting scheme for the complex claim (thesis) of the discovery argument. State the warrant scheme in Column 10. Write the thesis statement for the discovery argument in Column 11.

Analyzing the Argument

Once you have completed the literature survey and mapped and outlined the argument for "What is known?" evaluate its soundness using Exercise 4.2.

Figure 4.12 Literature Survey Tally Matrix: Stage 3

Stage 3. Analyze the patterns of the data.			
	Simple claim statement (premises) (9)	Warrant scheme and complex argument (10)	Complex claim statement (11)
	Simple claim placement as an evidence statement for the major claim	Warrant scheme used to justify the complex argument	The thesis for the discovery argument
Author Text Periodical (A)			
Author Text Periodical (B)			
Author Text Periodical (C)			
Author Text Periodical (n)			

EXERCISE 4.2

Evaluating an Argument

Evaluating the complex argument

1. What is the complex argument for your thesis?

2. What premises make up the complex argument?

3. How are the premises warranted to conclude the thesis?

4. What is the logic scheme of your argument? What reasoning pattern is used (cause and effect, side-by-side, chains)? Is the complex argument logical?

5. Is anything out of place? Are there simple claims that are irrelevant to the argument? Note them. Avoid both "red-herring" statements that provide off-topic information, and "rabbit-run commentary" that strays from the subject of the topic by following tangential information.

Evaluating the simple argument

1. Are your simple claims soundly reasoned? That is, do the simple arguments posed create a simple claim supported by evidence and a valid warrant?

2. Is each claim properly supported by evidence?

3. Is each of the simple arguments correctly warranted by sound reasoning patterns that justify each claim made?

4. Are there any disconnected claims or evidentiary statements? Do they need warranting or discarding?

TIPS

- Make sure that you have completed a comprehensive search before beginning your literature survey.
- Use some form of tally matrix to storyboard your arguments. The tally matrix is both an organizational and a critical thinking tool. Whatever form you use, be sure to take advantage of both features.
- The reasoning patterns are critical to assembling good arguments. Learn them so they will be available to you as needed.

Summary

The literature survey is the discovery of what is known about the subject of research. To conduct a literature survey, first develop a tally matrix to examine the data; and then conduct a final check on the truth of the evidence collected. Next, organize and group the data entries from the tally matrix into evidence to develop the claims. Build the groups chronologically, thematically, or in combination. Once you build the groups, you can compose the reasoning patterns and maps to create simple arguments. Build and organize simple claims into the premises of the major argument. You are now able to build the discovery argument (Figure 4.13).

Figure 4.13   Survey of Literature: Argument of Discovery

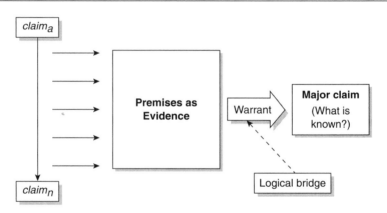

Given the data on the subject, this is what we know . . .

You have now completed the literature survey. The argument of discovery for what is known about the subject of research is in place. The first argument, or the front end, of the research case is done. However, what are the implications of what is known about the research subject? Does what is known about the research subject answer your original inquiry? Are there gaps, omissions, debates, and questions about the topic that need further study? Given what is known about the subject of the research, what can you conclude? These are all questions that ask you to critique the present knowledge on the topic. We address the second argument that is needed to complete the research case in the next chapter.

CHECKLIST	
Task	**Completed**

Assemble the Data
- Create survey tally matrix. ☐
- Catalog and document major works of recognized importance. ☐
- Build author lists. ☐
- Catalog citations. ☐
- Organize data into categories by theme. ☐
- Bracket main ideas by theme category. ☐
- Review the quality and strength of the data. ☐

Synthesize the Data
- Organize core maps and outlines according to theme patterns. ☐
- Create historical log of scan process. ☐
- Revise tentative author maps, subject maps, maps by theme and by main idea bibliographic entry card abstracts, and notes to construct evidence categories. ☐
- Apply a warrant scheme to each theme group. ☐

Analyze the Claims
- Examine maps and tally matrix to formulate a complex argument scheme. ☐
- Outline the discovery argument. ☐
- Apply a warrant scheme to the discovery argument. ☐
- Build complex arguments and major claims (this is your thesis statement). ☐
- Do an explanatory write. ☐

Critique the Literature

Interpreting the Research

Botte buona fa buon vino.
A good cask makes good wine.

The Literature Review Model

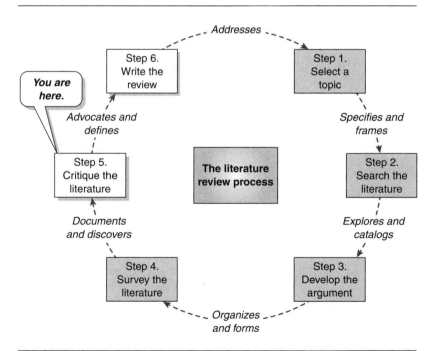

C ritiquing is the art of interpreting the meaning of a piece of literary, scientific, or technical work. A critique consists of a well-founded argument that stems from a detailed analysis and assessment of that work. A *literature critique* interprets the current understanding about the topic of research and determines how this knowledge answers your research question. When conducting the critique, ask, "What is the answer to the research question I have posed, given what I now know about the subject?" If the answer is clear and is defined by the discovery argument, you have found the thesis for your literature review. The literature review has met its purpose, a thesis concluded from a synthesis of current knowledge about the topic.

Most class assignments and master's studies expect this level of inquiry. Projects such as doctoral dissertations and some master's theses, however, demand extending topic knowledge beyond what is known by uncovering a question for original study, a *research problem.* You must ask more questions: "What added, original research would extend present knowledge?" "What are the gaps, contradictions, omissions, and debates about the research subject surfaced by the discovery argument?" In a doctoral program, the literature critique must go further than supporting what is now known about the subject. Here, too, you must develop an *argument of advocacy* that defines what is known. Also, you must define the unanswered question, the question that needs new primary research.

Whether it is a thesis that interprets what is known about the study topic or a thesis that surfaces a new problem for research, you must present a sound argument of advocacy that justifies your thesis.

Stage 1. Implicative Reasoning

The literature critique argument uses implicative reasoning to reach a conclusion. **Implicative reasoning**, by definition, is a logical interpretation of evidence to produce propositions that signal a specific conclusion. If A is true, then we can assume that B is also true. The literature critique argument uses claims made in the argument of discovery as propositional evidence to advocate the thesis of the literature review. The literature survey and literature critique arguments appear in sequence making an "if . . . then . . ." case.

Here is a simple example of an "if . . . then . . ." case. "If it is raining, then you should take an umbrella when walking to work." Notice there are two arguments in this statement: "if it is raining" and "take an umbrella." Each of the arguments has two independent claims that need separate proofs. The first statement, "If it is raining," needs proof that it is raining. Once it can be proven that rain is falling, it is necessary to propose that it would be reasonable to take an umbrella to work. Does the need for an umbrella logically follow? The warrant of the first case (direct observation) comes from using some means of observation to confirm that it is raining. The proven claim that it is raining becomes the premise for the evidence of the second argument. "Given that it is raining, what should you do?" The second argument must logically argue the implications of the facts to settle on a reasonable action. This argument must show that, because it is raining, you will get wet walking outside. If you prefer to stay dry, you should use an umbrella. The backing for the warrant's force is that previous experience has demonstrated that the use of an umbrella can protect a person from the rain. The warrant provided the logical bridge to justify the use of an umbrella as a reasonable conclusion. This example may seem an exercise in overexplanation. However, breaking down each of the steps of this example shows the analytical reasoning used when employing an "if . . . then . . ." case.

Stage 2. The Two Arguments

Use "if . . . then . . ." arguments to connect the claims from the literature survey (Step 4) to the conclusions eventually drawn from the literature critique (Step 5). Express these linked arguments as follows: "*If* this is what we know about the subject of research, *then* the following implications can be concluded given the research question." These implied conclusions become the thesis statement of the literature review. Chain reasoning is the logical pattern for developing the "if . . . then . . ." arguments that make up the literature review case. Use a chain reasoning pattern, as discussed in Chapter 4, to diagram the two arguments for a research case. These arguments form a storyline that can be logically mapped as shown in Figure 5.1.

Figure 5.1   The Literature Review Case

$$\begin{array}{cc}
\text{(If)} & \text{(Then)} \\
\textit{Discovery argument} & \textit{Advocacy argument}
\end{array}$$

$$(R_1 \ldots R_n \therefore C_1) + (C_1 \therefore C_2)$$

The (If) argument presented in Figure 5.1 depicts the discovery argument made in the literature survey (Step 4). Here you use evidentiary data as reasons to determine what is known about the subject of study. The claims made in the discovery argument are intermediate by nature and link to the advocacy argument that will become the premises. The claim C_1 of the first argument of the chain becomes the premise C_1 of the second argument of the chain. They now become the foundational evidence for the literature critique argument.

Looking at the (Then) argument of the diagram in Figure 5.1, you use the premises stating what is known to answer the original question posed by the study. If X is known about the subject, then how does X answer the research question? The result is the argument of advocacy that produces the conclusion of the case, C_2, the thesis statement of the literature review.

Figure 5.2 describes how chain reasoning builds an "if . . . then . . ." connection to build the arguments that make the case for the literature review.

Figure 5.2 presents the two arguments that compose the case for the literature review. During the literature survey, you built the argument of discovery. During the literature critique, you build the argument of advocacy. Notice that complex claims justified in the argument of discovery are the foundational evidence for the advocacy argument of the literature critique.

The argument of advocacy is an "if . . . then . . ." argument. If the major claims found by the argument of discovery are true, then you must conclude the following answer (thesis) to your research question. Because the argument of advocacy is implicative, the warranting pattern must justify its implication. As seen in the "if rain, then umbrella" example used earlier in this chapter, the implicative logic of experience warrants carrying an umbrella to work. That experience used an ends and means reasoning pattern for its justification. "If it is

Figure 5.2 The Research Case of the Literature Review

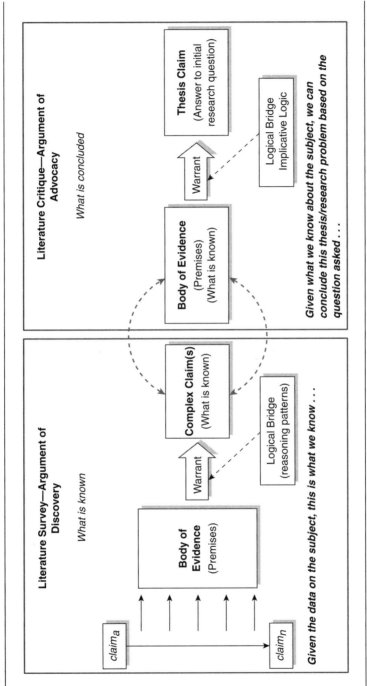

raining and we want to remain dry, experience suggests that using an umbrella is a suitable means to satisfy that end." As with this example, your argument of advocacy must also use the complex claims found by your argument of discovery to answer your research question. Your success in supporting your thesis depends on the implied logic used in your argument.

Stage 3. Argument Patterns

To build the argument for the literature critique, ask the following question: "If the premises stating what is known about the research question are X, then what can I conclude?" To begin to answer this question, you must identify the connection between the known premises and the research question itself. What information is the study question looking for? How do the premises answer the question? What logical link makes the "if . . . then . . ." connection? Ehninger and Brockreide, in their text *Decision by Debate* (1960), identified nine basic patterns as warranting schemes for the implicative argument. These nine patterns identify the links between the study question and the claims made by the argument of discovery. A sound rule of logic forms the basis for each pattern. Select the argument pattern that provides the best logical connection between premises and the thesis (conclusion).

The key to selecting the correct pattern is to see the linkage between the answer the research question is seeking and the evidence and premises developed by the literature survey. For instance, let's begin with a simplified research question. "What eating habits lead to obesity in children?" The information needed to answer this question is causal to the effect of obesity. The best fit for a logical link is a cause-and-effect connection. Since the question states the effect and asks for the causes, then the argument of discovery must provide premises that state the eating and activity habits that can lead to obesity. Figure 5.3 shows how to apply these basic logic patterns when developing the advocacy argument for a literature critique. Following the chart is a summary, with examples, of the nine implicative patterns of logic used to form the literature critique argument. Each pattern connects to a rule of logic and the prerequisite condition you must show to fulfill the needs of the arguments.

Figure 5.3   Nine Patterns of Argumentation

Argument pattern	Rule of logic	Prerequisite conditions: "The researcher must show that . . ."
Cause and effect	For every cause there is an effect.	. . . the body of evidence identifies data that are directly causal.
Effect to cause	Every effect has a cause.	. . . the body of evidence contains the direct effects caused by the case defined in the research question.
Sign	Identifiable symptoms, signals, or signs precede events and actions.	. . . the data identified by the body of evidence are symptomatic of the action or event defined in the research question.
Sample to population	What is true of the sample is also true of the whole.	. . . the sample identified in the body of evidence is truly representative of the population defined by the research question.
Population to sample	What is true of the population is also true of a representative part of that whole.	. . . the sample defined by the research question is actually representative of the population identified by the body of evidence.
Parallel case	Where two cases are similar, what is true of the first case is also true of the second.	. . . the case identified in the body of evidence is similar enough to the case defined by the research question to make them parallel.
Analogy	Because two items are alike, a conclusion drawn from one can be assumed to be a conclusion drawn about the other.	. . . the case identified by the body of evidence contains qualities that provide explanation or clarity to similar qualities contained in the case defined by the research question.
Authority	The more a person knows about an issue, the more factual the claim about that issue.	. . . the testimony presented in the body of evidence uses reliable expert testimony relevant to the case defined by the research question.
Ends–Means	The result is directly attributable to performing a named action.	. . . the action identified in the body of evidence of the literature survey will achieve the ends as identified by the research question.

1. *Cause and effect.* Causes lead to effects is the implied rule of logic that warrants this pattern. To use this argument, you must show that the body of evidence premises the causes of the effects defined in the research question.

   Research questions using this argument pattern are these:

   - "What are the reasons for the high school dropout rate among inner-city minority teens?"
   - "What are the causes of multigenerational welfare dependency?"

   Each question defines an effect and asks for the causes. The premises settled by the discovery argument must provide the causal evidence that leads to the thesis argument.

2. *Effect to cause.* The effect to cause pattern uses the reverse logic of cause and effect. The rule states that all effects come from a cause or causes. You can use this pattern when you can show that a body of evidence defines the effects caused by the case defined in the research question.

   Typical research questions falling within this argument pattern are these:

   - "What are the effects of early intervention programs on teen alcoholism?"
   - "What is the impact of hard-line contract negotiations on employee morale?"

   These research questions state a cause and ask what resulted from that cause. The premises created from the discovery argument must provide the evidence of the effects that lead to the thesis argument.

3. *Sign.* The sign pattern works when the research question is seeking legitimate signals, indicators, or symptoms of an event or action. The rule of logic supporting this pattern is that actions or events are preceded by symptoms, signals, or indicators. The precondition for use of this pattern must show that the premises are the legitimate symptoms, signals, or indicators of the case as defined by the research question.

   Research questions using this argument pattern are these:

   - "What are the early warning signs of autism in children?"
   - "What are the qualities of a dysfunctional group?"

Each of these research questions demands premises that provide signs or signals applied to the condition identified in the research question. The premises then become those qualities, and you can claim them. The premises concluded from the discovery argument must provide the symptoms, signals, or indicators as evidence that leads to the thesis argument.

4. *Sample to population.* When the question of inquiry examines a representative sample of a defined population to decide the qualities of that population, use the sample to population pattern. The rule of logic that warrants the connection states that what is true of the sample is also true of the whole. It is critical that the sample identified in the body of evidence actually represent the population defined by the research question. Thus, the rule stating that what is true of the sample is also true of the population provides the logical connection that ties the premises to the conclusion.

   Research questions using this argument pattern are these:

   - "Based on the SAT results of the past ten years, are California high school graduates better prepared to attend university than all other high school graduates from all other states?"
   - "Are students attending universities sponsored by the American Bar Association (ABA) better prepared than students attending universities that are not sponsored by ABA, based on first-time passage rate for students taking the bar examination?"

   Each of these research questions needs data about a population and about the sample under examination. To apply this pattern, you must be able to show that this sample is actually representative of the population. Claims must use representative samples of the identified population as evidentiary data. When you have met the rule of logic, the premises will show a logical conclusion (thesis) about the population.

5. *Population to sample.* Population to sample applies when the research question seeks to define or describe a sample or predict its actions using data about the general population. The rule of logic states that what is true of the population is also true of a representative part of that whole. This argumentative

pattern uses the reverse logic of the sample-to-population argument. In this argument, the premises represent the qualities of an entire population and apply to the sample identified by the research question.

Research questions using this argument pattern are these:

- "What interpersonal communication skills are used by health professionals to build cooperative client behavior?"
- "What leadership strategies are employed by managers to foster employee commitment and cooperation?"

Both of these questions seek premises drawn from evidence about an entire population that is directly attributable to the sample in question. This pattern of argumentation works when the characteristics of the whole are drawn directly from the representative sample. To use this type of argument, you must show that a sample defined by the research question is actually representative of the population identified by the body of evidence.

6. *Parallel case.* Many research inquiries ask for comparisons about two identified cases. This pattern works to make the critique argument when the two cases are similar. The parallel case pattern uses the comparison of two like cases for its logic. The rule for the parallel case is that, where two cases are similar, what is true for the first case is also true for the second.

Research questions using this argument pattern are these:

- "What teaching strategies employed in selected high-performing schools can be used by other high-performing schools to increase student competence in science?"
- "What interpersonal skills employed by a sample of effective executive teams can be used by other effective executive teams to promote positive communications?"

Each of these research questions uses the likeness of the qualities of the exemplary case as the premise to address the case defined by the research question. To employ this pattern, you must show that a case identified by the body of evidence is similar to the case defined by the research question.

7. *Analogy.* Use an analogy argument when a research question seeks to clarify or expose the qualities of a particular case by

comparing it to an archetype, a prototype, or a stereotype. The analogy argument also uses the logic of comparison. The analogy pattern compares like parts within a defined case to parts within a prototypical case for purposes of explanation or clarification. This comparison differs from the parallel case in that the parallel case argues the likeness of the two cases. The analogy argues that qualities or parts contained in each of the cases are similar.

Research questions using this argument pattern are these:

- "How can institutions compare to the model of a living organism to explain their internal workings?"
- "How are the steps of building a literature review like assembling a jigsaw puzzle?"

The previous questions signal the use of an analogy argument. To employ this pattern, you must show that a case identified by a body of evidence clarifies and explains something not understood by relating it to what is familiar.

8. *Authority*. Reference to authority is the most common pattern used in forming a research question. The logic employed depends on reliable expert testimony or observation that directly applies to the case defined in the research question. The rule of logic states that, since the expert finds the case to be true and the expert is a valid source, then it is true.

    Research questions using this argument pattern are these:

    - "What is the nature of human intelligence?"
    - "What are the characteristics of effective leadership in complex organizations?"

    These questions can effectively use relevant expert testimony as evidence to justify the conclusion, the thesis of their case. To employ this pattern, you must show that a case identified by the body of evidence provides the authoritative answer to the question posed by the research question.

9. *Ends-Means*. The research question that asks for a preferable direction, method, or action to take uses the ends-means pattern to form the critique argument. The rule of logic employed states that a result is directly attributable to carrying out a chosen action. In this pattern, the direction or action

claimed by the premises will achieve the end sought in the research question.

Research questions using this argument pattern are these:

- "What interactive skills must a trainer have to conduct a productive third-party intervention?"
- "What coaching skills are necessary for mentors to work successfully with first-year interns?"

In each of the previous questions, look for propositions that offer the solution to the issue posed by the research question. To employ this pattern successfully you must show that the action identified in the body of evidence of the literature survey is designed to achieve the ends as identified by the research question.

Each of these nine patterns provides a logical rule that justifies the premise (evidence) to the claim (conclusion), thus satisfying the basic rules of argumentation. The previous nine reasoning patterns provide the means to warrant the conclusion for an argument of advocacy, the thesis statement of the literature review. Each of the patterns provides a logical rule that justifies the premise (evidence) to the claim (conclusion), thus satisfying the basic rules of argumentation.

STAGE 4. BACKING

Before leaving the patterns of implicative reasoning, consider one more important notion: backing the warrant. Assume a reasonable implicative pattern developed the argument, but a question remains: Is the pattern legitimate? Each of the reasoning patterns has a rule of logic that makes it operable. Each relies on this rule as a specific condition that you must fulfill to use the pattern correctly. For example, when applying the population-to-sample pattern, the rule states that what is true of the population is also true of a representative part of the population. For a researcher to apply this pattern correctly, two preliminary conditions are necessary to satisfy the underlying rule. These two conditions provide the backing that makes the pattern valid.

- First, the part identified must be a valid sample of the population under study.

- Second, the part identified must be a representative sample of the population under study. Representative means the sample represents all qualities of the population.

Without meeting these conditions, the rule of logic that forms the pattern is not usable. Each of the nine patterns has one or more conditional rules that are necessary for using the argument pattern correctly. Toulmin, in developing his argumentation theory, calls these conditional rules the backing for the warrant. Backing provides confirmation for the warrant. Figure 5.3 provides the backing rules and preconditions necessary for each of the nine basic implicative argument patterns.

By employing the proper argument pattern to create the logical connection between the research question and the premises formed in the argument of discovery, you can build an argument of advocacy and logically warrant the thesis of your literature review.

Building a strong case for the thesis is a major concern for every researcher. While the thesis case will never be perfect, it must be sound. This means that your case, when presented, must be able to withstand rebuttal arguments made against it. Soundness also implies that a community of peers can understand and accept the case premises and thesis.

We will use the example given in Chapter 4, "History of the Theory of Intelligence," to explain building a literature critique. A map of that argument using the argument for discovery model appears here (Figure 5.4). This map shows how you were able to address the question "What is the definition of human intelligence?"

When examining the far-left column of Figure 5.4, you can see that this researcher collected the various major theories on human intelligence by theoretical contributors. Notice that, in the center column of the figure, the theoretical perspectives fell within two camps when the researcher tallied the data to develop the body of evidence. The researcher used a complex warranting scheme, building arguments of side-by-side reasoning, to organize the simple claims into the evidence supporting each major theory. Divergent mapping shows two major theoretical camps that were in opposition. This complex reasoning scheme then became the warrant for asserting the claim that two prominent theoretical positions on the nature of human intelligence were claimed in the twentieth century. The far-right column of Figure 5.4 shows the major claim.

Figure 5.4   Twentieth-Century Cognitive Perspectives: Argument of Discovery

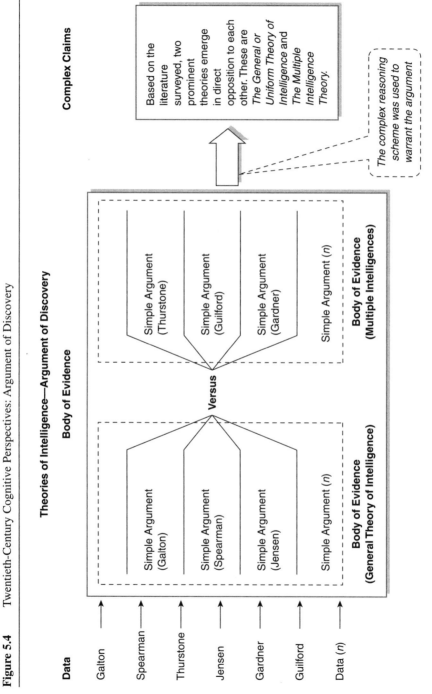

Theories of Intelligence—Argument of Discovery

Data

Galton
Spearman
Thurstone
Jensen
Gardner
Guilford
Data (n)

Body of Evidence

Body of Evidence
(General Theory of Intelligence)

Simple Argument
(Galton)

Simple Argument
(Spearman)

Simple Argument
(Jensen)

Simple Argument (n)

Versus

Body of Evidence
(Multiple Intelligences)

Simple Argument
(Thurstone)

Simple Argument
(Guilford)

Simple Argument
(Gardner)

Simple Argument (n)

Complex Claims

Based on the literature surveyed, two prominent theories emerge in direct opposition to each other. These are *The General or Uniform Theory of Intelligence* and *The Multiple Intelligence Theory.*

The complex reasoning scheme was used to warrant the argument

The major claim that was a product of the argument of discovery from the literature survey now becomes the premise used to develop the argument of advocacy. Figure 5.5 depicts how the second argument supports the thesis of the case.

When framing the argument of advocacy, begin by restating the study question originally framed as the research interest. The thesis of the literature review must address this question. In this example, the research question is, "What are the prominent theories addressing the nature of intelligence from a cognitive perspective that were postulated during the twentieth century?" The thesis of this researcher's literature review must answer this question. The researcher must assemble and argue the current understanding about the prominent cognitive theories dealing with human intelligence in a way that successfully answers the question. This work begins by presenting what is known.

Beginning with the left-hand columns of Figure 5.5, the researcher transfers the claims made in the argument of discovery to the premises of the argument of advocacy. These claims are now the supporting evidence used by the researcher to make the argument in response to the study question. In the example, a synthesis of the premise states, "Based on the literature surveyed, two prominent theories emerge in direct opposition to each other. These are the General or Uniform Theory of Intelligence and the Theory of Multiple Intelligences." The data provided to support this premise are the evidence supplied by the simple claims presented in the argument of discovery.

At this point, the researcher has stated the current knowledge about the question posed. Do the premises stated answer the study question? When applying the premise to the study question, it becomes obvious there is a satisfactory response. Twentieth-century psychologists postulated two significant theories about the nature of human intelligence. Does this information properly respond to the study question? If so, which seems likely, the literature review presents evidence addressing the research question. However, is the claim or thesis statement warranted? What makes this evidence believable? Here, the researcher must review the divergent reasoning pattern (see Chapter 4) to justify the reliability and truth of the premises. At that point, the researcher can successfully argue that these premises are reliable and valid.

Figure 5.5 Twentieth-Century Cognitive Perspectives

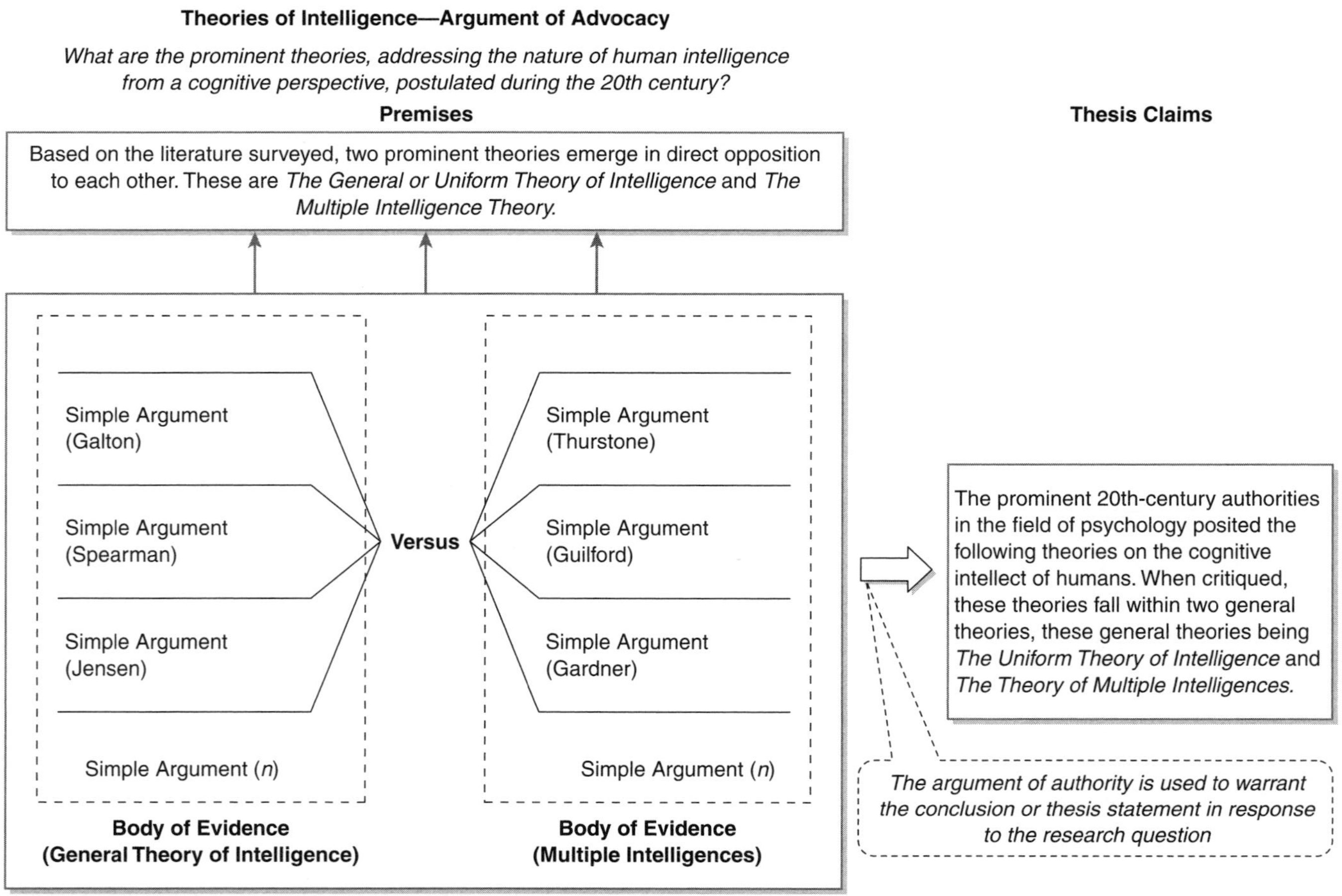

Theories of Intelligence—Argument of Advocacy

What are the prominent theories, addressing the nature of human intelligence from a cognitive perspective, postulated during the 20th century?

Premises

Based on the literature surveyed, two prominent theories emerge in direct opposition to each other. These are *The General or Uniform Theory of Intelligence* and *The Multiple Intelligence Theory*.

Thesis Claims

The prominent 20th-century authorities in the field of psychology posited the following theories on the cognitive intellect of humans. When critiqued, these theories fall within two general theories, these general theories being *The Uniform Theory of Intelligence* and *The Theory of Multiple Intelligences.*

The argument of authority is used to warrant the conclusion or thesis statement in response to the research question

Body of Evidence (General Theory of Intelligence)

Simple Argument (Galton)

Simple Argument (Spearman)

Simple Argument (Jensen)

Simple Argument (*n*)

Versus

Body of Evidence (Multiple Intelligences)

Simple Argument (Thurstone)

Simple Argument (Guilford)

Simple Argument (Gardner)

Simple Argument (*n*)

What logic allows the researcher to assert that because the various authors have claimed these theoretical principles, their testimony provides a justification for asserting the thesis? The researcher uses an implicative argument of authority to justify the thesis, as shown in the right-hand column of Figure 5.5. The researcher states the thesis: "The prominent twentieth-century authorities in psychology proposed the following theories on the cognitive intellect of humans. When critiquing, the thesis claims present two general theories: the Uniform Theory of Intelligence and the Theory of Multiple Intelligences."

To make the implicative connection between the premises built into the argument of discovery, the researcher examined the nature of those premises and found them built on authoritative evidence. Reasoning from authority makes good sense since the body of evidence is well grounded by expert testimony. Thus, by using this pattern as a warranting scheme, the argument of advocacy asserts a rational conclusion. However, the critique can continue further. Notice that evidence that supports the premise comes from divergent mapping. The researcher's responsibility is to present the rebuttal cases made by each of these opposing views to further explain and qualify the thesis statement. To complete the literature critique, the researcher must present the points and counterpoints of the debate. At the end of this evaluative discussion, the researcher might even decide that one of the theories is more convincing than the other. The researcher might also consider the possibility of extending the current knowledge about the research subject by developing a new research question that would suggest original research to provide an answer to the current debate.

EXERCISE 5.1

Evaluating Your Literature Critique

Use the following when you review your literature critique. Examine your own work to evaluate its strength.

1. Review your original study question. Do the premises built in Argument 1 provide a satisfactory answer to the research question? If not, what work do you need to do next? If the answer is satisfactory, then the premises lead directly to declaring the thesis.

(Continued)

(Continued)

2. Examine the nature of the evidence presented to support the premises in answering the study question. Is the evidence based on cause and effect, effect to cause, sign, sample to population, population to sample, parallel case, analogy, authority, or ends-means? Often more than one pattern might fit. If so, select the pattern that makes the most persuasive argument. Compose the thesis statement or research problem. Ensure that you have support for the case of the argument pattern.

3. Build the critique discussion. In support of the thesis, analyze and evaluate the premises and body of evidence built into the argument of discovery to further clarify the key ideas offered by the thesis. For example, this critique could entail modeling key parts, an evaluation of the debate, a clarification of the omissions and gaps in the current knowledge, or the definitional development of the thesis.

STAGE 5. FALLACIOUS ARGUMENTS

Beware of the pitfall of **fallacious arguments**, which are arguments leading to a mistaken or misleading conclusion. As seen earlier, the lack of convincing data, inappropriate or disconnected evidence, and unwarranted claims can all lead to a fallacious argument. The two most common fallacies in argumentation are jumping to conclusions and overlooking alternative explanations.

When a researcher asserts a conclusion based on skeletal evidence, the risk of jumping to a faulty conclusion increases. Building a fallacious argument by jumping to a conclusion can also be caused by an incomplete evaluation of the evidence.

The second great temptation for the researcher is to bias the argument by presenting a conclusion without properly addressing other alternatives. Researchers rarely have a one-sided argument. When such a case seemingly presents itself, usually the researcher either was blinded by a preferable conclusion! or did not delve deeply enough into the data to find alternative possibilities. Avoiding these temptations will help ensure research strength and is a great defense against committing the two most common fallacies of argumentation.

Here are some of the other major fallacies researchers must avoid.

- Research that engages in *name calling* attacks data, a position taken, or an expert by impugning the personal character of the author.
- Research that appeals to *emotions* bases its argument on an emotional rather than an evidentiary position. It makes its appeal to the crowd or draws its conclusion based on group-think rather than building a rational case for its conclusion.
- Research that appeals to *ignorance* uses the logic that a claim must be true because it has not been proven false. This back-door logic for proving the existence of a claim is simply wrong.
- *Misplaced causality* often occurs when research uses the arguments of cause to effect, or effect to cause. As shown earlier, to prove causality you must ensure an irrefutable connection between the action that causes and its incumbent effect. Too many researchers argue causality without considering other actions or events that could have a bearing on the connection.
- Research that *begs the question* occurs when it asserts a claim and uses that claim as the evidence for the assertion. This is circular reasoning, as in "There is a God because God said so."
- Research that reaches a *disconnected conclusion* does so without evidence to support it. Either there is no evidence presented to back up the claim or there is no connection between the evidence presented and the claim proposed.
- Research that reaches an *"everybody knows that"* conclusion appears to make a case where none exists. Here, the researcher draws a conclusion based on some ill-defined or vague notion of a case. No evidence is presented, neither expert testimony nor observation. Instead, the researcher bases the claim on false premises or on opinion.
- Research that results in the *loaded question* has formed a research question that contains one or more false or questionable presuppositions. The classic example is, "When did you stop beating your wife?" Notice that this question is fraught with presupposition. It assumes that you have a wife and that you beat her. These assumptions assume facts without the backing of any supporting evidence. The researcher commits this fallacy when composing a research question in which one or more of the key concepts depend on unproven presuppositions that propose a truth but that lack authentication.

- Research that *poisons the well* biases the argument by using controlling language. Here the researcher uses descriptive language to sell the argument either negatively or positively without respect for the evidence. An example is, "This study examined the effects of the bureaucratic, authoritarian, and wasteful *No Child Left Behind* program had on the reading achievement of third-grade inner-city children in California."

There are many other fallacious arguments. The ones mentioned above are a few of the more common ones that you might meet. Remember, making strong arguments of discovery and advocacy is the best way to avoid fallacious arguments.

STAGE 6. THE CASE IS EVERYTHING

The thesis case is the critical part of any literature review. Unless it presents a sound case that backs up its thesis, a literature review fails to meet its purpose and lacks any credibility. Presenting the case, the soundness of its arguments, and the clarity of its logic are the primary concerns of the literature survey and the literature critique. When building a literature survey and a literature critique, the researcher must constantly decide whether you are making a case correctly. The thesis of any study is only as good as the case that supports it. As the Italian proverb puts it, "Botte buona fa buon vino."

TIPS

- The literature critique is the last impression left with your readers. Make sure it is forceful and defendable.
- After your literature critique is complete, review the figures in Chapter 5 as a means of checking the case you have built.
- Review your arguments to identify the reasoning patterns you have used. Do they meet the preconditions?
- Check the list of fallacies to be certain that you have not fallen prey to any of them.

SUMMARY

Chapter 5 explains how to create the argument of advocacy necessary to support the case for the literature review. It deals with the purpose of a literature critique and the three steps necessary to complete this task. Using "if . . . then . . ." logic as the foundation for the thesis, the chapter shows the connection between the discovery and advocacy arguments. The nine linking patterns provide avenues for building strong, implicative logic between the research study question and the premises that warrant the thesis of the study. A good literature critique must not only prove the advocacy argument, tying what is known to what can be concluded, but it must also provide the necessary evidence to describe fully the implications of that thesis. Finally, the chapter supplies a list of common fallacies that can become pitfalls of good argumentation.

CHECKLIST	
Task	Completed
Reviewing the Topic Question	
1. Analyze the question framed as the basis of the study.	☐
2. Decide which implicative warrant type is inferred by the study question.	☐
Building the Advocacy Argument	
1. Build the premises from the complex claims of the discovery argument.	☐
2. Organize the premises with a suitable warrant scheme.	☐
3. Build the advocacy argument.	☐
4. Build the thesis statement.	☐
5. Compose an exploratory write on the advocacy argument.	☐

Write the Review

Write, Audit, Edit

Scribendi recte sapere est principium et fons.
The secret of all good writing is sound judgment.

—*Horace*

The Literature Review Model

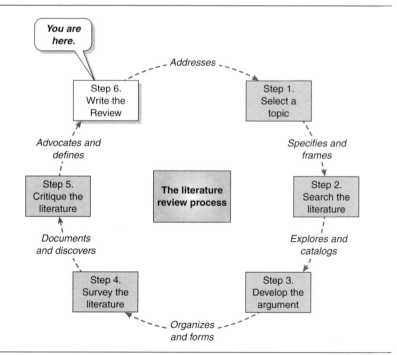

Y ou have completed your research and developed a research case. Your background information is organized and mapped, and your evidence is cataloged and documented. You have interpreted, analyzed, and developed arguments and done some exploratory writing. All of the pieces are at your fingertips. The task is simple now . . . or is it? Some students believe that all they need to do is assemble the research information and begin typing, but formal writing does not begin with composing the first draft. Far from it.

Writing your thesis demands that you deliberately create, mold, and refine your data. It starts with imagining how your end product will look. Then through revision—which involves composing, auditing, and editing—the work evolves into a final polished composition. Good writing develops in two stages: in Stage 1, writers write to understand; in Stage 2, writers write to be understood (Figure 6.1). You first write as you learn what you want to say; then you write as you learn how to say it.

Figure 6.1   The Writing Process

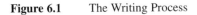

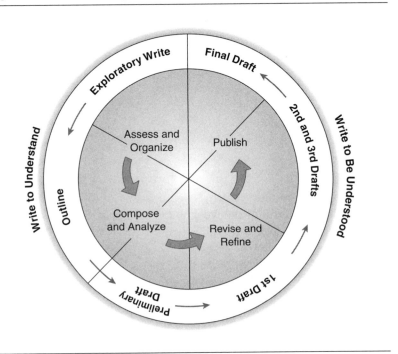

If you want to write to understand, you first must become immersed in the subject matter. A deep understanding of the material gives you the ability to think critically about it. Only after you can fluently discuss the subject without referring to your notes can you begin to write. You start with exploratory writing and creating an outline, then working through a preliminary draft. Writing to be understood starts with crafting a series of drafts, then auditing and editing each until the composition tells a story that others can hear. You first learn what must be said and then learn how to say it. These two stages contain specific tasks. Figure 6.1 shows the stages and tasks of the writing process.

THE WRITING PROCESS: OVERVIEW

Writing evolves through two major stages: writing to understand, and writing to be understood. Each stage includes tasks that develop and refine the work resulting in a final draft suitable for publishing.

Stage 1. Write to Understand

Task 1. Exploratory writing. The first task is to write an exploratory composition to develop and assess your knowledge of the subject. The exploratory write provides an evaluation of how well you understand and can orchestrate the contents of the work and exposes any gaps in thinking or research documentation.

Task 2. Outline. The next task is to compose a formal outline of the work. The outline sequences and forms the subject material for composition.

Task 3. Preliminary draft. A preliminary draft that is the first detailed rendition of the work is the next task. Edit this preliminary draft for accuracy and continuity.

Stage 2. Write to Be Understood

Task 1. First draft. The edited preliminary draft provides the basis for writing the first draft, which is the first effort at writing to be understood by an audience.

Task 2. Second draft. See Task 3.

Task 3. Third draft. The second and third drafts follow specific editorial strategies to further refine the work.

Task 4. Final draft. The revisions in Tasks 2 and 3 produce the final or published draft. In this task, you build, organize, refine, and revise ideas into a clear and logical body of work.

You first write, then audit to find errors and omissions, then edit to correct and revise the work (Figure 6.2).

After writing comes auditing, which is an inspection of the recently completed work. When auditing an outline or draft, check and align the content, and proofread it carefully. The purpose of the audit is twofold: it must uncover all flaws in the work and assess the success of the draft in meeting its intent.

When editing, you adjust the content and flow of the composition and correct its organization and grammar. The product of the edit is a revision of the previous composition. The writing, auditing, and editing tasks continue throughout each stage of the writing process, refining the work until the project is completed.

Figure 6.2   The Iterative Tasks of Writing

Stage 1. Write to Understand

Writing to understand is a formative act of learning and owning the subject matter. First, you must gather and organize the ideas that make up the research content. You must assimilate, arrange, and form these ideas into a well-articulated design for composition. The act of composing begins with summing up and transforming the threads of data into a new, original, cohesive expression of that data. You must create the pattern of the story, weaving the threads of each idea together to form the composition. Only you can do this. Remember the example of the jigsaw puzzle? When assembling the puzzle, the puzzle maker looked at the picture on the box to see how the pieces fit together. The writer, too, must see a picture of the subject matter to create clear writing. If this mental image is not created, the writing will not form. How is this image created?

Assimilating the subject matter into personal understanding begins with subject comprehension. Next, as the writer works with the material, original ideas and patterns emerge. Finally, you thread these patterned images together to create new meaning that becomes the foundation of the written composition. Writing to understand occurs through the tasks of exploratory writing, outlining, and preliminary composition.

Exploratory Writing

Creating Writing Readiness

You are an outside observer when conducting research. Gathering data, identifying evidence, and building a case are all exercises in working with others' ideas. While personal knowledge of the subject grows throughout the research work, it is still recall, remains abstract, disjointed, and untested. You are dependent on notes, outlines, and maps. The subject material must be internalized. You are no longer the outsider noting and recording ideas, but are now the critical insider creating and composing new meaning.

The Literature Review

To have command of the subject knowledge, you must study the material as if you were preparing for a final exam. Pretend you are going to teach this material to a group of students. Do you know it well enough to teach it to a class? Is it organized in your mind? Can you anticipate questions about it? If the answer to any of these questions is no, you need to spend more time on preparation.

Most writers know that writing is the great arbiter of their knowledge. They cannot write what they do not know. When beginning to write, this fact becomes painfully clear. To write successfully on any topic, you must learn it so thoroughly that it becomes a familiar friend. Unless you first thoroughly learn the material, you are trying to sew a garment with thread but no fabric.

Ask yourself two questions.

1. What do I actually know about my subject?

2. How will I explain it to someone else?

Exploratory composition provides the opportunity to test your familiarity with, and understanding of, the research. Without the aid of support or background material, write what you know about your research. The following is a guided exercise in this first task under Stage 1.

EXERCISE 6.1

Guided Exercise for Exploratory Composition

Directions: This composition should come from the top of your head. Do not use any notes or supporting materials. Write a paper of no more than five pages responding to the following questions.

1. What is your topic?

2. What do you know about the topic?

3. What is the context or background surrounding the topic?

4. How is this topic significant?

5. What is your central claim or thesis?

6. How can you prove it?

7. What conclusions have you drawn, and what reasons support them?

8. What are the implications of your research for the field?

When you have completed this paper, put it down and leave it for several days. After returning to the paper, check your readiness for writing a literature review. Use the following audit questions to discover your familiarity with the subject. If you need to review the materials, refer to the chapters as noted.

1. Have you accurately defined the topic and its core concepts? (Chapter 1)

2. Is the topic clear and concise? (Chapter 1)

3. Have you described the general issue or concern that inspired the topic? (Chapter 1)

4. Have you identified the academic area of your approach, and is your language recognizably the language used in that academic field? (Chapter 1)

5. Does this topic clarify your original interest? How does the topic respond to the interest? (Chapter 1)

6. Does your evidence show that this study is important to the field? (Chapter 1)

7. Do you have a sound argument of discovery for what is known about the topic? (Chapters 3 and 4)

8. How does the argument of advocacy address the problem? (Chapter 5)

9. What is the proof or evidence for your thesis? (Chapter 5)

10. Based on your thesis, do these conclusions resolve the problem or question prompted by your first interest? (Chapter 5)

11. Do your conclusions and your arguments work as a unified case, a compelling whole? (Chapter 5)

After studying your guided writing and the audit question responses, what more do you need to know about your topic? This is an opportunity to take stock of your efforts and to decide whether it is time to move forward or if you first need to go back and gather more information to build a better personal understanding of the research case.

Outline

The audit of the exploratory composition can create an immediate compulsion to write. Resist this urge. The ideas, threads, and patterns that emerged from your exploratory composition must first be arranged into a well-organized, cohesive, and complete body of knowledge. You must ensure that all the pieces of the puzzle are present and in their right places. This is a time for analysis and reflection. Producing an outline allows you to carry out this necessary task.

Outlining, the second task in writing to understand, is the tried-and-true method for beginning the formal development of the composition. The outline serves as an organizer that documents your thinking about the research. Here you wed the personal intent and perspective created in the exploratory write to your researched information forming a comprehensive profile of the subject. Outlining serves three purposes. It acts as (a) a mechanism for integrating and transforming ideas, (b) a mechanism of sequencing those ideas, and (c) a general plan for the composition.

a. As an integrating mechanism, the outline provides a way to transform your research into a story. When outlining, you are constantly moving subject knowledge from a cursory understanding of another's work to an intimate personal understanding of the subject. The reflective thinking needed forces you to shift from collecting and reporting ideas to knowing those ideas, analyzing them, and interpreting them. Thinking through an outline transforms your perspective from observer to participant in the storytelling process.

b. Outlining also acts as a sequencing mechanism. When forming the outline, you must organize information, arrange ideas, and create the threads and patterns for the composition. You must articulate your concrete ideas, place these ideas into logical sequences, and build logical patterns to combine these sequences into cohesive patterns of thought. An outline constantly demands that you reflect on what information has come before, what information is currently being included, and what information logically comes next. The outline is a record of the idea sequence and the road map for writing.

c. Finally, the outline is the general plan for the literature review composition. It sketches the overall design and notes the essential features of the work. Think of an outline as the blueprint for a house you are building. The outline provides a design plan for the written composition. It both clarifies the big picture and provides the specific dimensions for each of the parts or sections of the written work.

An outline, like a blueprint, shows the overall design of the work. It also specifies the dimensions, the exact content of the composition. Review the completed outline for specificity. Does it provide clear direction and enough information to allow you to advance with a minimum of second-guessing and rethinking? Does it provide a sound overall design? Does it include all the details necessary to support developing the design?

When building the outline, start by creating a table of contents. Create a frame for the composition by laying out the major sections of the work in a logical fashion. The three major parts for the literature review are the introduction, the body, and the summation. The *introduction* provides a profile of the study. Its purpose is to engage the reader by presenting highlights of the essential parts of the work. In the *body*, you present the case and document it to justify the research thesis. Finally, the *summation* gives a summary of the research study's conclusions. The introduction, the body, and the summation are subdivided into subject sections.

The Introduction

There are six basic sections in the introduction: (a) the introductory statement, (b) the study topic statement, (c) the context statement, (d) the significance statement, (e) the problem statement, and (f) the organization statement.

a. The *introductory statement* draws the reader into the work. It can be a poignant example, the essence of a debate on the question, or the question posed by the study. A narrative hook to grab the reader's attention serves to encourage the reader to continue reading by playing on emotions, attitudes, or beliefs. Consider this example: "Local school boards have abandoned the constituencies that put them in office. They have elected instead to become cogs in the wheels of state bureaucracies. Today, school boards are simply apparatchiks of the state." This example contains three powerful claims. They aim to elicit an emotional response from the reader that should create a continued interest in reading the work.

b. The *study topic statement* defines the subject of the research. This section should be a concise statement identifying the key ideas of the research. It should state the focus and perspective taken in addressing the topic. This section should clearly define each of the key ideas of the topic statement. The topic of study statement should be no more than two or three paragraphs in length.

c. The *context statement* addresses the study's setting. It recounts the circumstances that surround, and perhaps have created, the research problem. These can be academic debates or concerns. The circumstances could also be practical issues or problems that have led to studying the problem. The context statement should provide information that defines the research problem's environment.

d. The *significance statement*, or needs statement, provides the justification for the study. This section recounts the writer's personal interest in the subject of study and provides documentation justifying the study's value to the academic community. The value of the research study may address a practical problem needing a solution or an academic issue that needs clarification or resolution.

e. The *problem statement*, or thesis question, is the question that needs to be answered by the research study.

f. The introduction ends with an *organization statement* that provides the reader with a thumbnail sketch of what will be presented in the literature review's body and summation.

The Body

The body of the literature review presents the case for the thesis in two sections: (a) the discovery argument, and (b) the advocacy argument. First, the *discovery argument* states what is known about the topic of study, and gives the background of the study. Second, the *advocacy argument* states the argument that leads to the thesis conclusion. This section develops the thesis. When outlining this section, you note the claims, evidence, and justification for each of these arguments and the case that justifies the thesis. This section also reports the research products of the literature survey and the literature critique.

a. The background of the study tells the story. Here you outline the arguments made for what is known about the topic of study. The literature survey tally matrix and the argument of discovery (Figure 6.3) serve as the major references for building the background statement. These aids are foundation resources. They document and catalog the claim statements, supporting evidence, suitable citations, and warrant justification necessary to build the argument for what is known. Use these reference aids as organizers to develop the background statement. The reasoning pattern made for the argument of discovery becomes the profile for the outline sequence. The major parts of the reasoning pattern become the headings and subheadings of this section of the literature review. The information contained in the literature survey tally matrix provides the necessary data to build the details into the outline.

b. The second task develops the thesis argument. Using the conclusions of the background statement as the starting point, outline the implications of what is known to address the research problem. The literature critique developed the contents for this section.

Use the literature survey tally matrix and the research case for the literature review model (Figure 6.4 on page 139) as the references for outlining the thesis argument. The implicative logic pattern used to justify the thesis argument is the basis of the outline. Again, the major claim, supporting simple claims, evidence, and citations can provide the details for this section of the outline.

The Summation

This section of the literature review summarizes the thesis argument. It is made up of (a) the thesis statement, (b) the thesis analysis, and (c) the study's implications.

a. The summation section begins by restating the research thesis.

b. Next, the analysis provides a detailed interpretation and explanation of the thesis. Here you can note an explanation of the key ideas of the thesis, provide further definition to those ideas, and explore the thesis from various perspectives.

Figure 6.3 Major Reference Aids

	Stage 1 Assembly					Stage 2 Synthesis			Stage 3 Analysis		
	Key concept or Descriptor (1)	Citation or Reference (2)	Main Ideas (3)	Data Quality (4)	Evidence Categories (5)	Warrant Scheme—Simple Arguments (6)	Simple Claim Statement (7)	Claim Acceptability (8)	Simple Claim Statement Grouping (Premises) (9)	Major Claim Statement (10)	Warrant Scheme Complex Argument (11)
	Taken from maps and Bibliographic Entry Card	Taken from maps and Bibliographic Entry Card	Taken from maps and Bibliographic Entry Card	Do data meet quality standards? (yes or no)	Data Entry placement into a body of evidence	Warranting scheme used for this evidence group	Data Entry is evidence for following claim	Does claim meet acceptability standards? (yes or no)	Simple claim placement into a complex argument	Premise is evidence for following major claim	Warranting scheme used for this complex argument
Author/ Text/ Periodical (A)											
Author/ Text/ Periodical (B)											
Author/ Text/ Periodical (C)											
Author/ Text/ Periodical (n)											

claim_a ... claim_n

Premises as Evidence → Warrant → Complex claim (What is known?)

Logical bridge

Given the data on the subject, this is what we know …

Figure 6.4 The Research Case of the Literature Review

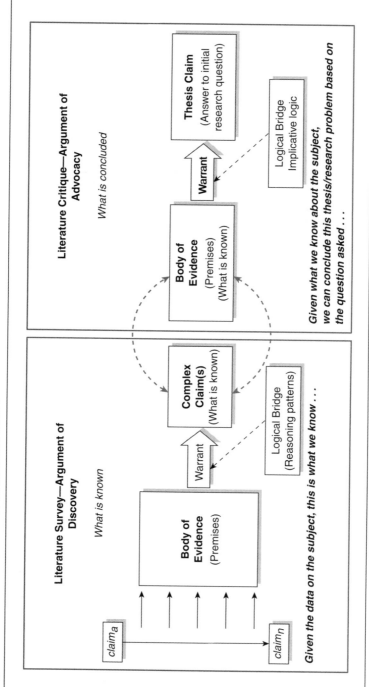

c. Finally, the implications state the impact of the thesis on the practical everyday issue or academic question that motivated the research study. In this section you note how the thesis solves the problem of the study.

Figure 6.5 shows the major parts and sections of a literature review. It also provides a listing of the study aids, maps, and references that can help build an outline for a review. The chapter references are listed for the reader's convenience.

Once you complete the outline, you should leave it for a day or two. After suitable time for reflection, thoroughly review the outline to ensure that it is complete, properly sequenced, and clear enough to provide a map for your written composition.

- Does the outline flow from one main idea to the next in a reasoned fashion?
- Does it thoroughly capture the contents?
- Are the claims made supported by strong evidence?
- Are all the conclusions warranted?
- Do the thesis points flow logically from one to the next?
- Does it represent an integrated whole?

Rework the outline until you can answer each of these questions affirmatively. Proofread your work. Review it not only for errors but also for its depth, connectivity, and continuity. Make the necessary corrections, and be alert for any mistakes.

Some Common Outlining Mistakes

To make your outline as useful as possible, avoid the following common errors.

- Resist the urge to compile just a list of facts and ideas. Listing quotes and ideas randomly is easy to do. While such a list might provide relevant details, it cannot provide the connections and theme for the written work. A list does not project the overall picture.
- An outline must include all the pertinent information that you amassed by doing research. Failure to include all the relevant ideas will result in an incomplete outline, which can only lead to an incomplete composition.

Figure 6.5 Literature Review Outline: Study Aids, Maps, and References

Major parts	Sections	Study aids, maps, and references	Chapter reference
Introduction	Introductory statement	Narrative hook	Chapter 6
	Study topic statement	The first library visit exercise	Chapter 1
	Context statement	Defining a specific research interest	Chapter 1
	Significance statement	Survey in literature, argument of discovery model, literature survey tally matrix	Chapter 4
	Problem statement	Argument of advocacy	Chapter 5
	Organization statement	Mapping schemes, reasoning patterns, argument of discovery and advocacy models, the exploratory write	Chapters 3, 4, 5, & 6
Body	Discovery argument	Mapping schemes, reasoning patterns, survey in literature—Argument of discovery model, literature survey tally matrix	Chapter 4
	Advocacy argument	Literature survey tally matrix, argument patterns, research case of a literature review model	Chapter 5
Summation	Thesis statement	Research case of a literature review model	Chapter 5
	Thesis analysis	Research case of a literature review model, literature survey tally matrix	Chapters 4 & 5
	Study implications	Defining a specific research interest . . . research case of a literature review model	Chapters 1 & 5

- Writer overconfidence, or overreliance on personal retention of the subject matter, can result in an outline that is either too brief or too vague. In this case, the outline does not provide enough descriptive detail to provide a clear understanding of the material. A brief or vague outline lacks queuing specificity.
- The outline should not be a shorthand version of the preliminary draft. There is a tendency to include too much information when writing an outline. This will produce too many fine details, which will soon obscure the big picture. Remember, the outline builds the blueprint but not the house.

How can you avoid these mistakes? Remember, your outline should provide the directions for writing the document. When building the outline, ensure that all the information is assembled. Spend time reflecting on your material so you can produce the cognitive structures and content themes necessary to build the story line.

Composing Drafts

Writing requires the creation of a series of drafts until the final composition emerges. Many years ago, a close friend of ours, Tim Cahill, then an aspiring young author, casually reflected on his writing. "Writing is a lot like having a baby. You go through months of pregnancy. The baby grows. You experience frustration and elation, depression and expectation. There is labor. You work hard. The baby is born. I feel like I am pregnant when I write."

Writing is the conception, gestation, and maturation of an idea. First, ideas must be conceived and brought to the page. Once they arrive, they must be formed into something that will communicate with the reader. They must be molded and polished to create the written representation of what had been imagined by the mind's eye.

The vehicle that carries you through this transformation is the draft. Drafts are not just rewrites: They are evolutionary documents that bring the writing from first formation to final rendition. Drafts are products of purposeful writing episodes that craft the writing, bridging the gap between Stage 1 (writing to understand) to Stage 2 (writing to be understood).

Each draft has a specific purpose. These tasks have rules of engagement, whether they are rules of composition, or grammar, or syntax. The tasks are sequential to allow the writing to flow and mature. As you move from one draft to the next, revise the writing. Drafting the work means revision that creates, molds, and finishes the written piece. When beginning to write, consider these suggestions.

- Reserve a quiet place for uninterrupted writing. Have comfort foods available if you need them, but don't make the writing place so comfortable that you become sleepy.
- Ensure that you have writing reference and support materials at your disposal, including an authoritative thesaurus and dictionary. Often, the essence of a word or the synonym of a word will escape you as you write. These texts will help you to get the right idea on paper.
- Good writing cannot be done in fifteen-minute spurts. Ensure that you have a significant block of time to get into the work so ideas flow. Do not think about blocks of times in minutes but in hours and days.
- Find your time for writing. Is it in the early morning, or the late evening? Each of us has a time of day that lends itself to our best writing production. For many, it is the early morning, when the mind is fresh and rested and you are less likely to be interrupted. Develop a regular schedule for your writing. A regular schedule will allow you to maintain the flow and pace of the writing.
- Schedule periodic breaks within your writing session. Give yourself time to stretch and reenergize, and then return to work recharged.
- Set a minimum page count as a goal, and achieve that goal. Concentrate on writing the ideas and producing the text.
- Have a plan about what you will write during the session. Create a mental picture of the piece. See its main ideas and its details.

The Preliminary Draft

Outlining organizes your thinking. Next, you must expand the outline into coherent sentences, complete paragraphs, and a cohesive composition. The preliminary draft is the first test of your true understanding of the material. What do you actually know about the subject? Can you express that knowledge in writing? Answering these questions is the task of a preliminary draft. This draft is the first try at narrating concrete statements in sequence. The task of the preliminary draft is to transfer your thoughts and ideas about the subject to paper.

The strategy for creating the preliminary draft will vary depending on your writing ability and content knowledge. Use the recommended strategy for framing any draft: write, audit, and edit. When composing a draft, first write it based on the intent and purpose of the draft. Next, audit the writing for content, sequence, composition, grammar, and cohesiveness. Finally, edit to fill in gaps and correct mistakes.

The preliminary draft has three major objectives:

a. First, determine how to write the story.

b. Next, transfer the early mental model of the subject into a concrete form.

c. Finally, check your knowledge of the subject.

Writing the preliminary draft may seem daunting. Take it one task at a time, building it in sections. Use the outline to decide how to arrange the writing; then develop your composition one brick at a time. Choose a section, and begin writing. When engaged in the preliminary write, write everything you know about that section or topic. The ideas will transform themselves as they leave the abstract and take the concrete form of the written word. Ideas will flow in randomly and in spurts. Try to order them while keeping the flow of the writing. Work at being concrete and sequential in your thinking. Take time to make the ideas form. Give the ideas definition and clarity. Do not overthink or overwork an idea at the expense of losing the next idea. Remember, you will have the chance to polish your work later when you audit it.

Are you unsure of a word or idea? Refer to the dictionary. Dictionary definitions can help clear up mental blocks and ambiguity. Dictionary definitions can also help in providing the keys to the right wording. Are you searching for the right word to express an idea? Use your thesaurus. Synonyms are helpful for expressing your exact ideas. Are you unsure of what comes next? Play, scratch, doodle, or put words on paper. Eventually, the next idea will show up. If not, step away from the writing, take a break, get some fresh air, and then return recharged.

Preliminary Draft: The Audit

The purpose of this audit is twofold: First, it aligns your first rendition of the work with the subject outline; second, it controls the revisions in content and composition needed to create a coherent body of work. The steps used to audit the preliminary draft follow:

1. Before you audit the draft, allow at least two to three days, or preferably a week, to pass. This time enables your mind to erase the mental picture formed when writing the draft and will allow you to see the work with fresh eyes and an open mind. You will be surprised at what appears: dangling ideas, misplaced thoughts, sentences without meaning, vague language, and lapses in logic. What you thought was a good piece of work may reappear as a primitive work in progress.

2. Begin the draft by triple-spacing the work. The extra room will give you room for additions and notes. Next, print it out; many things that "disappear" on the screen are glaringly obvious on paper. Next, read the work aloud. Hear the words and thoughts as if you were hearing them for the first time. Note any incongruities, redundancies, and omissions.

3. As you read, audit the content of the work. Check for a consistent flow of ideas. Look for gaps in logic and knowledge. Review for the correct sequence of ideas. Ensure that proper transitions link major thoughts. Make sure that each paragraph has a beginning, a middle, and an end. Finally, insert corrections where you need to cite evidence.

4. Once you complete the content audit, audit for grammar, composition, and style. Check for grammar usage. Look for misused words and phrases. Check punctuation and spelling. Check for continuity of person, the use of active voice, and word economy. Again, correct any errors as you go. The seminal reference used to guide this step of the audit is *The Elements of Style* by Strunk and White.

5. Complete the preliminary audit by aligning the draft to the subject outline. Place the written outline and the corrected draft side by side. Track the outline contents to reconcile the two. What needs adding, removing, or clarifying in the draft?

You may need to refer to the tally matrix or other research references to align the draft. Make any necessary changes. Now is the time to insert the needed citations in your style.

6. When you finish the audit, reread for a global view of the work. Check for content integrity and logic. Look for incomplete ideas. Ensure that you make suitable transitions. Double-check the order and the sequence of ideas.

Preliminary Draft: The Edit

After the audit is complete, you need to revise. Using the marked-up copy of the draft created by the audit, rewrite the work. Make the line-by-line changes you noted. As you make changes, reread the sentence or paragraph for correctness and clarity before going on to the next. Continue until you finish the entire draft. Read the revision aloud to ensure that everything is in place. Your ear will pick up errors and bumpy spots that your eye missed. Reading your writing silently allows your mind to substitute what you meant to say for what is actually on the page. Make any corrections needed.

The edit of the preliminary draft completes the transfer of subject knowledge to your consciousness. You now own the subject matter. The audit of your preliminary draft has forced you to develop the subject ideas into an original body of work. By auditing and editing the composition, you have cleanly penned it to paper. One question remains. Is the work understandable to others?

STAGE 2. WRITE TO BE UNDERSTOOD

Writing to be understood is the act of drafting and redrafting the work into a finished piece that accurately and adequately communicates the subject ideas to others. Does the composition tell the story as you intended? Have you told the right story? Is the story told being heard? You are now writing for an audience. Essential to this undertaking is a partnership with others in the mutual crafting of the work. A useful discussion with others about the form and content of the work provides the direction for each revision. Based on the problems uncovered through the outside review, you can refine the work for clarity, continuity, and content integrity.

Each draft is a developmental revision of the work. At this stage, each draft should evolve, making the picture more complete, more consistent in flow and voice, and more accurate in depicting the subject. You should be asking, "Do you see what I see? If not, what must I change to bring the picture into focus?" With each revision, you mirror the changed work back to selected members of your audience through auditing and editing until you have the finished product you want.

The focus of the first draft is to produce a clear, written communication and to gain audience understanding. The preliminary draft provides a strong foundation for building a first draft. To ensure that the best rendition of the work goes to others to review, complete one last reading of the preliminary draft checking to ensure the following:

1. Are syntax, voice, and paragraphing in alignment?

2. Is the grammar correct?

3. Is the piece written in active voice ?

4. Is the point of view consistent (first or third person)?

5. Are verb tenses consistent (present or past)?

6. Are paragraphs well formed and aligned?

Double-check for accuracy and strength of evidence and the integrity of the case you are arguing. Alec Fisher, in his text *The Logic of Real Arguments* (2003), suggests an easy way to check the integrity of arguments you developed to make the thesis case of the work. The following exercise is based on this method. You might find it a helpful tool in preparing the first draft.

EXERCISE 6.2

Analyzing the Research Arguments and Case

The purpose here is critical analysis of the research arguments that make up the thesis case. You will identify all the parts of the research case and evaluate them to decide the validity of the research thesis. Analysis and

(Continued)

(Continued)

evaluation are your two major tasks. First, analyze the piece of work to check the following:

- The main conclusions of the research are clear.
- The claims and evidence that support each conclusion are in place.
- The form and logic of each argument are stated or clearly implied.
- Each argument is warranted.

Second, evaluate the work to decide if the following are true:

- The logical reasoning is acceptable.
- Suitable warranting supports the arguments' conclusions.
- The overall argumentation makes the thesis case.

Analysis

1. Review the paper and look for the claim statements. Underline them.

2. Review the paper again and look for evidence statements. Circle them.

3. Look for warrant statements for the argument and its simple claims and connect them to the proper claim and evidence statements. Use connecting arrows for this task. If warrant statements are implied, state them in the margin where the claims and evidence are presented.

4. You have now combined the claim, evidence, and warrant statements for each of the simple claims and the complex claims of the research piece. Place a box around each argument.

5. Review the simple claim arguments. Are they correctly formed? If not, note the problem areas, and revise them.

6. If the claims or arguments are incomplete, rewrite them.

Evaluation

1. After completing the analysis, evaluate the arguments. Do they make the case? Begin by evaluating the major thesis statements.
   - Are the simple claims connected to a major thesis?

- Are the simple claim arguments connected? Does the logic scheme of each argument work? Are the simple claims linked as cause and effect statements or perhaps as daisy chains?
- Does the logic of the major argument make rational sense? If you find simple claim arguments that do not fit the logic scheme of the major claim, make adjustments.
- If you find interesting fact statements that are irrelevant to the argument, remove them. Red-herring statements and rabbit-run commentary may be interesting information, but their inclusion into the argument scheme weakens the argument.

2. If you find the logical plan for the thesis argument lacking, revise it. Consider what warrant scheme can best link the simple claims into a pattern that will build the thesis arguments. Then revise as necessary.

3. Does the research piece make its case?

Have your outline, logic maps, and tally matrix available for this exercise. They provide the necessary information for a quick alignment of the logic sequences.

This exercise provides a sound tool for analyzing and evaluating your research arguments. It should show the integrity of the arguments and provide an overall assessment of the quality of the research theses. Identify the specific areas of strength and weakness in your research and correct them as needed. Once you have finished the first draft, it is time to send it out for auditing.

Outside Review

Taking drafts to an audience is a central part of each part of Stage 2. For the writing to be understood by others, you must view the writing from an audience's perspective. Each person sees the world from a unique logic and vantage point. Your perspective is not necessarily seen by others. Since you are writing to be understood, you must transform the writing into language and logic that are effectively understandable to others. The outside review is crucial to this transformation. You must give serious thought to the plan for outside review before moving to the first and following drafts. Here are a few points about selecting outside reviewers and drafting to be understood:

- Select outside reviewers for their expertise in the field. Choose some for their competence as writers and editors, and choose others for their subject expertise. Ask each to review the work carefully and to give you a comprehensive response. The more specific and comprehensive the response, the better the revision. Remember, you are looking for a thoughtful, useful critique that adds value to the work, not a pat on the back.
- When preparing the draft for review, provide specific directions to the reviewer. Highlight areas that may need work. Assure your readers that they should employ their expertise in critiquing the piece. Have all reviewers comment on the readability of the work. Triple-space the draft to provide enough commentary space. Use line numbers for easy reference. To avoid confusion, date and number each draft.
- Set up a timetable for the return of the draft. Make time to review the returned drafts carefully. Arrange a time to discuss the returned drafts with each reviewer.
- Complete the auditing with all reviewers before moving to the second and third drafts. Integrate the revisions suggested by the reviewers. Clear up any conflicts between reviewers to your own satisfaction, then edit.

The Second and Third Drafts

The edited first draft has transformed the composition into a work that is understandable to an outside audience. The purpose of the second and third drafts is to refine the clarity and precision of the text so the work becomes the best rendition you can produce. Most changes made to the work now derive from specific audience response. Though you are writing for the large audience of scholarly peers, recognize that this audience is represented by a specific few who will vet the work. This audience is either the instructor who will grade the effort or a committee who reviews the work. Those who vet your work should provide the response necessary to polish these drafts and move them to the final published product. The goal of the second and succeeding drafts is to meet the expectations of those readers who are the arbiters and referees of the work. The key to the success of these later drafts is in the auditing you do to meet these expectations.

The Final Draft

Writing the Final Draft

Polishing the first draft is a matter of refining the work to meet the expectations of those who will approve the publication. When considering these later revisions, picture your audience. Think as they would think. Anticipate their standards for quality work. Revise your work from this vantage point. If a writer's guideline or rubric is available for such a purpose, review it carefully for suggestions and direction. Use these vantage points to revise the first draft. Begin by reading the draft aloud. Listen to what you say using the reviewer's perspective. Audit the manuscript based on any anticipated questions or concerns. Review the work again for content accuracy. Also make sure that you are up to date on current knowledge. Do a final check on the work's form and format by double-checking the approved style manual. Make revisions as needed.

Auditing the Final Draft

The guidelines used to conduct the audit of the first draft also work for polishing the later drafts. The audience changes for the refereed review. When auditing the second and succeeding drafts, have the instructor or committee review the work. Do this audit before the final submittal. If an instructor is grading the work, provide the polished draft for commentary. Provide plenty of time for the review. If a committee is responsible for approving the piece, work with the chairperson to develop a plan by which the committee can review the work and provide directions for suggested changes. Avoid surprises by refining the work to their specific expectations and specifications. Your task is simple: Make all suggested changes.

STYLE MANUALS

A literature review is a formal document. Specific rules of style dictate its publication form and format. Recently, we found more than 150 style manuals that guide the formal publication of research works in the United States. Each academic field has its particular presentation format. The use of these manuals can vary by university, school, department, or even classroom instructor or research chair. Turabian, APA, and MLA are the most widely used in the social sciences in the United States. Become familiar with the style manual required for your research project. Take the time to examine your required manual for a general understanding of the rules of publication. Know how you will format, organize, and write your project. Each manual has specific rules for these issues.

A style manual usually has the following sections:

- The parts of the manuscript. In this section you will find specific instructions about the front and back matter of your project. The information included specifies the format of your title page, copyright page, dedication or acknowledgment page, table of contents, and illustrations, among others.
- Text composition. This section will provide instruction about the style of your work. The rules of punctuation, spelling, use of numbers, quotations, captions and legends, tables, bibliographies, and references are explained.
- Rules for production. This last section will provide guidance on the formatting and form of the manuscript. The rules for formatting, pagination, headings, graphics, indent, production of figures, and tables, are found here.

The style manual is a reference work. After taking time to familiarize yourself with it, you will rely on it throughout the auditing and editing processes. When writing your preliminary draft, refer to your manual to set the correct format (font, margins, and so on) for the manuscript. When auditing the preliminary draft, ensure the text composition conforms to your style manual's directives. Audit the style again when you are preparing your first draft for outside review. To ensure that you are following the rules for publishing, refer to the style manual, as necessary, as you audit each successive draft. Finally, conduct a style audit for the last edit before formal publication.

TIPS

Some tips for writing follow:

- Start with the main idea, build its evidence, then summarize. After you have fully explored an idea, make sure there is a link (segue) to the next idea to bind the ideas and make a cohesive and coherent composition.
- In early drafts, write everything you know and want to say about the section of your topic. Do not stop to edit or rethink. Keep going.
- Initially, do not worry about grammar, spelling, or punctuation. Work at letting the ideas flow. The structure of the composition will be checked during auditing and editing.
- Use your notes and outlines sparingly. Work at producing the writing from your head rather than from your references.
- Do not leave the notepad or keyboard until you have completed each section.
- Try not to end the writing session until you have charted the work for the next session.
- Be patient; be inquisitive; and be relentless. Do not leave the work until you have it exactly as you want it. Then expect to go back to it and work it again.

LAST WORDS

By following the procedures discussed in this chapter, you can make the writing of a literature review a rewarding experience. The key to writing a successful literature review is to be deliberative. Build a strong outline as the foundation of the work. Make sure the outline lays out the design of the composition and has enough details to give you a useful design for writing. Develop the composition in stages, first writing to understand and then writing to be understood.

Begin by writing an exploratory draft to transform the research to your perspective. Reconcile the exploratory draft to the research outline. This will build a strong foundation for the preliminary draft. Use auditing and editing to direct the revisions necessary for creating a quality first draft. Remember, use others to audit and provide response to mold the work into a composition that can be understood and accepted by the intended audience. Writing the literature review is not a complicated art form. Rather, it is an evolutionary sequence of writing and revising, with each revision molding the composition until it tells the author's story with clarity and grace. The act of writing is not necessarily a joy; reading a well-written piece that you have worked through carefully is a joy. To have written is. For that reason, *Carpe diem, quam minimum credula postero.* Seize the day, and put no trust in the morrow! Get on with the writing, and tenaciously follow it wherever it takes you. Craft it well. Experience the joy of completing a good work, to understand and to be understood.

> *Writing a book is an adventure. To begin with, it is a toy and an amusement; then it becomes a mistress, and then it becomes a master, and then a tyrant. The last phase is that just as you are about to be reconciled to your servitude, you kill the monster, and fling him out to the public.*
>
> —Winston Churchill (from a speech
> about his World War II memoirs delivered
> to Britain's National Book Exhibition, 1949)

Glossary

Argument: The presentation of one or more claims backed by credible evidence that supports a logical conclusion.

Argument of advocacy: An argument that is based on claims that have been proven as fact, which serve as the premises for logically drawing a conclusion, in this case the thesis statement of the literature review.

Argument of discovery: This argument proves that the findings-in-fact represent the current state of knowledge regarding the research topic.

Auditing: Making a thorough examination of a piece of writing to evaluate its errors and omissions.

Boolean query: A data search conducted using key words connected by the logical operators "and," "or," and "not" to define the specific area of interest.

Claim: A fact that is open to challenge.

Complex argument: Complex arguments consist of multiple claims that are formed to build premises that lead to a major thesis.

Core ideas: These are central ideas that provide meaning to the interest statement under study.

Data: Data are pieces of information.

Deduction: An inference in which the conclusion necessarily follows from the facts given.

Evidence: A set of data presented as the grounds for substantiating the claim.

Fallacious argument: An argument that leads to an erroneous or misleading conclusion.

Implicative reasoning: Logic which follows from an "if . . . then . . ." pattern, where the "then" part is true whenever the "if" part is true.

Interest: When you are working toward a topic, an everyday interest is an idea that comes from personal experience in the field, which becomes a research interest after being translated to the language of a particular academic discipline.

Key terms: Those words or phrases that control and define meaning.

Literature critique: As the culminating process of a literature review, a literature critique is a detailed analysis and assessment of current understanding about the topic of research, and how this knowledge leads to the thesis.

Literature review: A written document which develops a case to establish a thesis. This case is based on a comprehensive understanding of the current knowledge of the topic. A literature review synthesizes current knowledge pertaining to the research question. This synthesis is the foundation which, through the use of logical argumentation, allows the researcher to build a convincing thesis case.

Literature search: Collecting, cataloging, and documenting data which will determine salient works and which refines the topic.

Literature survey: Builds the argument about the current knowledge of the research topic.

Major claim: A major claim is based on the premises warranted by a complex argument. These premises are based on simple claims and their simple arguments.

Mapping: A means of graphically organizing data.

Premise: A previous statement of factor assertion that serves as the basis for a further argument.

Qualifiers: Data that demand rebuttal or concession and refute or limit the claim.

Scanning: Quickly reviewing material to determine appropriateness.

Skimming: Reading rapidly to acquire main ideas.

Simple argument: A simple argument is composed of a simple claim, its evidence, and its warrant.

Thesis statement: It expresses a conclusion based on a case developed using existing knowledge, sound evidence, and reasoned argument.

Topic: A research area refined by interest, an academic discipline, and an understanding of relevant key words and core concepts.

Warrant: The reasoning that is used in an argument that allows the researcher to accept the evidence presented as reasonable proof that the position of the claim is correct.

References

Booth, W. C., Colomb, G. G., & Williams, J. M. (1995). *The craft of research*. Chicago: The University of Chicago Press.

Churchill, W. (1949). *A speech about his World War II memoirs*. Delivered at Britain's National Book Exhibition, London.

Cooper, H. (1998). *Synthesizing research* (3rd ed., vol. 2). Thousand Oaks, CA: Sage Publications.

Ehninger, D., & Brockreide, W. (1963). *Decision by debate*. New York: Dodd, Mead & Company

Fisher, A. (2003). *The logic of real arguments*. Cambridge: Cambridge University Press.

Fisher, A. (2004). *Critical thinking: An introduction*. Cambridge: Cambridge University Press.

Hart, C. (2001). *Doing a literature search*. Thousand Oaks, CA: Sage Publications.

Hart, C. (2001). *Doing a literature review: Releasing the social science research imagination*. London: Sage Publications.

Kelley, D. (1998). *The art of reasoning* (3rd ed.). New York: W. W. Norton & Company.

Strunk, W., Jr., & White, E. B. (2000). *The elements of style* (4th ed.). New York: Longman.

Toulmin, S., Rieke, R., & Janik, A. (1984). *An introduction to reasoning* (2nd ed.). New York: Macmillan Publishing Co.

Toulmin, S. (1999). *The uses of argument*. Cambridge: Cambridge University Press.

Trimmer, J. F. (2004). *The new writing with a purpose* (14th ed.). Boston: Houghton Mifflin Company.

Weston, A. (2000). *A rulebook for arguments* (3rd ed.). Indianapolis: Hackett Publishing Company.

Williams, J. M. (1990). *Style: Toward clarity and grace*. Chicago: The University of Chicago Press.

Index

CORWIN
PRESS

The Corwin Press logo—a raven striding across an open book—represents the union of courage and learning. Corwin Press is committed to improving education for all learners by publishing books and other professional development resources for those serving the field of PreK–12 education. By providing practical, hands-on materials, Corwin Press continues to carry out the promise of its motto: **"Helping Educators Do Their Work Better."**